VISIONS
of ZION

VISIONS
of ZION

Alexander B. Morrison

Deseret Book Company
Salt Lake City, Utah

Library of Congress Cataloging-in-Publication Data

Morrison, Alexander B.
    Visions of Zion / Alexander B. Morrison.
       p.   cm.
    Includes bibliographical references and index.
    ISBN 0-87579-788-1
    1. Zion (Mormon Church)—History of doctrines.　2. Mormon Church—Doctrines—History.　3. Church of Jesus Christ of Latter-day Saints—Doctrines—History.　I. Title.
BX8643.Z55M67　　1993
230'.93—dc20　　　　　　　　　　　　　　　　　　　　93-36628
　　　　　　　　　　　　　　　　　　　　　　　　　　　CIP

Printed in the United States of America

10　9　8　7　6　5　4　3　2

Contents

v

Preface

This book is not an official publication of The Church of Jesus Christ of Latter-day Saints. No one asked me to write it, and I alone am responsible for errors or omissions in the text. The views and ideas presented herein are my own and do not necessarily represent the position or view of the Church.

All royalties received from the sales of the book have been assigned to the Church Educational System for African scholarship activities.

This book is dedicated to my dear children and to my wife, Shirley, whose purity of heart is a daily inspiration to me.

I am indebted to Stuart Reid and to Russell Osmond, who read the full manuscript, providing valuable suggestions for correction and addition, and to Lyle Cooper for his careful and expert reading of chapter 5. Carolyn Hyde typed, proofread, and corrected the manuscript with great skill. I have learned to always value her sound judgment and counsel.

Chapter One

"Zion, That Goodly Land of Promise"

The dream of a better world is as old as mankind. From time immemorial, men and women of faith and hope have dreamed of a Holy City, whose king is the Lord God Omnipotent; a place of refuge for the righteous fleeing the storms of a wicked world; an abode where peace is in every heart, where there is no fear nor want and all people are brothers and sisters, where faith and purity shine in every face. That place, in Judeo-Christian parlance, is called Zion.

Saints in our day as in other eras look forward to the establishment of Zion. "We will sing of Zion, kingdom of our God./Zion is the pure in heart,/Those who seek the Savior's part./Zion soon in all the world will rise to meet her God." (*Hymns,* no. 47.)

The Prophet Joseph Smith, for whom the vision of Zion was always near, stated that "the building up of Zion is a cause that has interested the people of God in every age; it is a theme upon which prophets, priests, and kings have dwelt with a peculiar delight." (*Teachings of the Prophet Joseph Smith* [Salt Lake City: Deseret Book, 1976], p. 231; hereinafter referred to as *TPJS.*)

EARTHLY ZIONS

A city called Zion existed long ago, in a day when "the Lord came and dwelt with his people, and they dwelt in righteousness." (Moses 7:16.) Enoch, their great prophet-leader, "built a city that was called the City of Holiness, even Zion. . . . And the Lord called his people Zion, because they were of one heart and one mind, and dwelt in righteousness; and there was no poor among them." (Moses 7:19, 18.)

Though Zion was blessed, the residue of the people were cursed by God because of iniquity. (See Moses 7:20.) Since Zion cannot abide with Babylon, in time the City of Enoch "was taken up into heaven. . . . For God received it [and its inhabitants] up into his own bosom; and from thence went forth the saying, Zion Is Fled." (Moses 7:21, 69.)

Though the City of Enoch is no more on earth, the dream of a Holy City lives on in the hearts of the righteous. "The Lord loveth the gates [i.e., the cities] of Zion more than all the dwellings of Jacob," sang the psalmist (Psalm 87:2), and the great Isaiah intoned, "In the last days . . . the mountain of the Lord's house shall be established in the top of the mountains, and shall be exalted above the hills; and all nations shall flow unto it. And many people shall go and say, Come ye, and let us go up to the mountain of the Lord, to the house of the God of Jacob; and he will teach us of his ways, and we will walk in his paths: for out of Zion shall go forth the law." (Isaiah 2:2–3.) Of that day the prophet declared, "They shall beat their swords into plowshares, and their spears into pruninghooks: nation shall not lift up sword against nation, neither shall they learn war any more." (V. 4.)

Though the righteous long for Zion, the concept of a Holy City, in impure hands, can and has been used for less than holy purposes.

Aurelius Augustinus, the Catholic St. Augustine, devoted thirteen years of his life to writing his masterwork, *De Civitate Dei* (*The City of God*), "the first great work to shape and define the medieval mind." Augustine divided all mankind into two camps: *Civitas dei* (the City of God) and *Civitas Terrena* (the City of the World). Where one chose to abide, said Augustine, would determine his or her ultimate destiny. "Mankind is divided into two sorts: such as live according to man, and such as live according to God. These we mystically call the 'two cities' or societies, the one predestined to reign eternally with God, the other condemned to perpetual torment with Satan." Theological details aside, Augustine clearly identified the church of his day with "the City of God," implying that the state, symbolized by *Civitas Terrena*, would be subordinate to the ecclesiastical power. We contend that the church of Augustine's day, the late fourth and early fifth centuries A.D., had already lost divine authority and was an apostate organization. No matter; for centuries Augustine's reasoning was used by ecclesiastical leaders, good and bad, to grapple for power with kings and emperors. (See William Manchester, *A World Lit Only by Fire* [Boston: Little, Brown, and Company, 1992], pp. 9–10.)

Over the centuries, all attempts by uninspired clerics and others to establish a "Holy City" have ended in abject failure. For example, radical Anabaptists tried to set up the New Jerusalem in the Westfalian city of Munster in 1534–35. Armed force was used, and a deluded character named Jan Bockelson went so far as to declare himself king over "the Kingdom of Zion." Troops of the local Catholic bishop stormed the city and, in a frenzy of blood and butchery, killed thousands, including Bockelson and the mayor of Munster. Many other Anabaptists in Germany suffered similar fates. (See Lewis W. Spitz, *The Protestant Reformation 1517–1559* [New York: Harper and Row, 1985], pp. 171–72.)

The lesson is clear: Zion can be established only with God's approval. Save His hand be in the work, it will fail. "Except the Lord build the house, they labour in vain that build it: except the Lord keep the city, the watchman waketh but in vain." (Psalm 127:1.)

The machinations of men aside, in addition to the Zion of Enoch's day, the dream of a "Zion Society" was fulfilled on one other occasion in human history. It occurred on the American continent in the aftermath of the visit of the resurrected Christ to the faithful Nephite remnant. So mighty were His teachings, so sublime His loving presence in their midst, that all the people, both Nephites and Lamanites, were converted unto the Lord, "and there were no contentions and disputations among them, and every man did deal justly one with another. And they had all things common among them; therefore there were not rich and poor, bond and free, but they were all made free, and partakers of the heavenly gift. And . . . there was no contention in the land, because of the love of God which did dwell in the hearts of the people. And there were no envyings, nor strifes, nor tumults, nor whoredoms, nor lyings, nor murders, nor any manner of lasciviousness; and surely there could not be a happier people among all the people who had been created by the hand of God. There were no robbers, nor murderers, neither were there Lamanites, nor any manner of -ites; but they were in one, the children of Christ, and heirs to the kingdom of God. And how blessed were they!" (4 Nephi 1:2–3,15–18.)

Sadly, after two centuries the American Zion was destroyed. Divisions, evils, false churches, pride, and persecutions arose; and the Nephite civilization tore itself apart in a paroxysm of blood and horror.

Although it didn't last long, one other society, following the mortal ministry of Christ, had some of the characteristics of a Zion Society. This fledgling society is referred to in conjunction with the day of Pentecost, when the Spirit was poured out in abundance. On that occasion, Peter "with many . . . words did . . . testify and exhort, saying, Save yourselves from this untoward generation. Then they that gladly received his word were baptized: and the same day there were added unto them about three thousand souls. . . . And all that believed were together, and had all things common; and sold their possessions and goods, and parted them to all men, as every man had need. And they, continuing daily with one accord in the temple, and breaking bread from house to house, did eat their meat with gladness and singleness of heart." (Acts 2:40–41, 44–47.)

WHAT IS ZION?

Is Zion, then, a place, a geographic entity? In a sense, yes. It is Enoch's "City of Holiness," to be sure; but the term refers also to other places wherein congregations of the righteous forsake the world and seek perfection in Christ and His gospel. The Prophet Joseph Smith declared, "The whole of America is Zion itself from north to south, and is described by the Prophets, who declare that it is the Zion where the mountain of the Lord should be, and that it should be in the center of the land." (*TPJS*, p. 362.)

During the Millennium, Zion will have two great centers of strength, two Zion cities: Jerusalem, the Holy City of the Jews, and a "New Jerusalem" to be built at a time when the Lord wills it, in Jackson County, Missouri. It, too, will be Zion. There will not, however, be an opportunity for all the righteous to live in the Zion city called the "New Jerusalem." Of them, the Lord, who is no respecter of persons, has said, "I have other places which I will appoint unto them, and they shall be called stakes, for the curtains or the strength of Zion." (D&C 101:21.)

Thus, Zion may be thought of in symbolic terms as a great tent with a canopy that covers the earth, supported by poles and cords and stakes. Isaiah spoke of the need to "enlarge the place of thy [Zion's] tent, and let them stretch forth the curtains of thine habitations: spare not, lengthen thy cords, and strengthen thy stakes." (Isaiah 54:2.) As such, Zion serves as a refuge from the wickedness of the world, a place where the righteous Saints of God may be sheltered from "wrath when it shall be poured out without mixture upon the whole earth." (D&C 115:6.) In a broad sense, Zion thus refers to the Church and kingdom of God "scattered upon all the face of the earth, and also among all nations." (1 Nephi 22:3.) As groups of the Saints in various locations grow in numbers and in their level of spiritual maturity, there comes the day when a new stake of Zion is established by priesthood authority. To that new part of Zion the righteous gather, and thus, steadily and surely, as the people become purified, "Zion . . . increase[s] in beauty, and in holiness; her borders . . . [are] enlarged; her stakes . . . [are] strengthened; yea, verily . . . Zion . . . arise[s] and put[s] on her beautiful garments." (D&C 82:14.)

This process of building and strengthening the great tent of Zion will continue until the dawning of the millennial day, when the King of kings will return in power and glory to dwell upon the earth. Then will the saints of God "break forth [in] joy" (Mosiah 15:30) as the scattered sheep of Israel gather to Zion and fulfill the marvelous millennial promises so long foretold by the scriptures. The New Jerusalem in America will have been built before that glorious Second Coming of Christ. To that Holy City will come Enoch of old and all his city. "And the Lord said unto Enoch: Then [that is, after Christ's Second Coming] shalt thou and all thy city meet them there [that is, in Zion, the New Jerusalem], and we will receive them into our bosom, and they shall see us; and we will fall upon their necks, and they shall fall upon our necks, and we will kiss each other; And there shall be mine abode, and it shall be Zion, . . . and for the space of a thousand years the earth shall rest." (Moses 7:63–64.)

EARLY ATTEMPTS TO BUILD A LATTER-DAY ZION

Early in this dispensation, the Saints tried on several occasions to build Zion in America. The first attempt to live the law of consecration and stewardship occurred in 1831 at Kirtland, Ohio. This was almost immediately abandoned, however; and those involved were sent to help build up the "City of Zion" in Jackson County, Missouri. Intense persecution drove the Saints out of Missouri in the late 1830s.

When the Saints migrated to the Great Basin following the martyrdom of the Prophet Joseph, attempts were again made to invoke the law of consecration in the 1850s and to set up the United Order in the 1870s. Human problems and frailties with which the Saints struggled as they attempted to live the United Order are illustrated by experiences at Orderville, established in 1874–75 in southeastern Utah. Many of the people in the Orderville United Order of Zion had come from the Muddy River Mission in southeastern Nevada, where they had nearly starved trying to raise cotton. Tempered in hardship, they had developed the camaraderie and sense of unity that come from the sharing of adversity together. At Orderville they laid out farms and built houses, a school, a communal dining hall and kitchen, a bakery, barns and sheds, and shops for carpenters, coopers, blacksmiths, shoemakers, and so on. Grains, cotton, fruits, and vegetables were raised and processed along with cattle, sheep, and poultry. A woolen factory was established. The group attained almost complete self-sufficiency. The Order prospered for several years before it began to unravel.

Some of the reasons for the ultimate failure of Orderville and of other attempts to set up Zion are illustrated by the following stories:

A certain young man of Orderville felt the need for a new pair of trousers. Unfortunately for him, his application for a new pair was denied; the ones he had were still serviceable. There was a big lamb crop that spring. The ingenious young fellow surreptitiously sheared the wool from the docked lambs' tails and when next assigned to take a load of wool to Nephi, took the lambs' tail wool with his load and exchanged it for a pair of store pants. His entrance at the next dance, garbed in his newly acquired sartorial splendor, reportedly caused a sensation!

The president of the Order demanded an explanation, which the young man truthfully gave. It was pointed out to the young man that the pants belonged to the Order and not to him. They would be taken, he was told, unseamed, and used as a pattern for all pants made in the future. He would have the first pair.

The tailoring department was soon swamped with orders for pants. Strangely, many boys reported that their old-style pants, produced in the Order's shop using coarse home-spun cloth, were wearing out, particularly on the seat. Some of the elders became suspicious. They noticed that the boys seemed to spend a lot of time in the shed where the grindstone was housed. Investigations showed that the boys were wearing out their pants on the grindstone! The elders protested but finally capitulated. A load of wool was dispatched to trade for commercially manufactured cloth. The tailor shop was soon a busy place. The pants rebellion was over; materialism, albeit on a minor scale, had won.

A certain sister of the Order washed and ironed clothes for miners at the nearby Silver Reef mines. Instead of turning the money she received over to the Order, she spent it on her children. A complaint was made to the bishop, but as she had always been a faithful worker, she was forgiven and told "go [to work] and sin no more." The lesson is plain: Zion cannot be built up by a people whose vision extends no further than me and mine. (See Mark A. Pendleton, "The Orderville United Order of Zion," *Utah State Historical Quarterly,* October 1939, pp. 141–59. For a detailed discussion of various attempts to build up Zion, including the Orderville experience, see L. W. Arrington, F. Y. Fox, and D. L. May, *Building the City of God: Community and Cooperation among the Mormons* [Salt Lake City: Deseret Book Company, 1976]).

Although persecution of the Church, both in Missouri and Utah, certainly did not favor successful implementation of the various attempts to build up Zion, it must be said that the Saints were not yet prepared to live a celestial law. Consequently, all the attempts failed, or at least fell short of their objectives. Though there were many individual exceptions, collectively speaking the hearts of the people were not pure; "they did not hearken altogether unto the precepts and commandments which [God] gave unto them." (D&C 103:4.) Because "they esteemed lightly [His] counsel" (D&C 101:8), the Saints suffered great afflictions at the hands of their enemies. The redemption of Zion has had necessarily to be delayed until the Saints, through chastening, learn obedience and are worthy to dwell in the perfect society that characterizes Zion. Oh, that we might have learned what Joseph Smith taught so clearly: "We ought to have the building up of Zion as our greatest object." (*TPJS,* p. 160.) Then would we honor the covenants given to prepare us for Zion!

> Behold, I say unto you, were it not for the transgressions of my people, speaking concerning the church and not individuals, they might have been redeemed even now.
>
> But behold, they have not learned to be obedient to the things which I required at their hands, but are full of all manner of evil, and do not impart of their substance, as becometh saints, to the

poor and afflicted among them; and are not united according to the union required by the law of the celestial kingdom; and Zion cannot be built up unless it is by the principles of the law of the celestial kingdom; otherwise I cannot receive her unto myself.

And my people must needs be chastened until they learn obedience, if it must needs be, by the things which they suffer. . . .

Therefore, in consequence of the transgressions of my people, it is expedient in me that mine elders should wait for a little season for the redemption of Zion—that they themselves may be prepared, and that my people may be taught more perfectly, and have experience, and know more perfectly concerning their duty, and the things which I require at their hands.

And this cannot be brought to pass until mine elders are endowed with power from on high.

For behold, I have prepared a great endowment and blessing to be poured out upon them, inasmuch as they are faithful and continue in humility before me.

Therefore it is expedient in me that mine elders should wait for a little season, for the redemption of Zion. (D&C 105:2–6, 9–13.)

Though the Saints failed in early attempts to establish Zion, it is well to keep their efforts in perspective. Although Orderville, for example, ultimately failed, many of its members looked back upon their experiences together as a time when they *nearly* realized the perfect Christian fellowship envisioned by the prophets. Historian Andrew Jensen, who visited Orderville in 1892, after its dissolution, wrote that the good Saints of Orderville gained an experience "that will never be forgotten by those who passed through it; and I was assured by several of the brethren who stuck to it till the last that they never felt happier in their lives than they did when the Order was in complete running order and they were devoting their entire time, talent, and strength for the common good. . . . Good feelings, brotherly love, and unselfish motives . . . characterized most of those who were members . . . until the last." (*Deseret News*, March 23, 1892, p. 4.)

Why did the Saints of the nineteenth century fail to establish Zion? Why did they fail to heed this divine commandment: "Thou art called to labor in my vineyard, and to build up my church, and to bring forth Zion, that it may rejoice upon the hills and flourish"? (D&C 39:13.) Why did they stop up their ears against this prophetic warning: "If Zion will not purify herself, so as to be approved of in all things, in His sight, He will seek another people; for His work will go on until Israel is gathered, and they who will not hear His voice must expect to feel His wrath." (*TPJS*, p. 18.) What were the abiding sins of our brethren and sisters that denied them promised blessings? Can we in our day learn from their shortcomings? Are their weaknesses our own?

It is fair to say that early attempts in this dispensation to redeem Zion failed primarily because of three abiding problems or weaknesses that sadly persist in our day. The Saints could not bring themselves to give up the things of this world; they were not united; and they were not willing to live the laws and commandments of the gospel. Since those who do not learn the lessons of history are condemned to relive it, it is instructive to consider, at least briefly, some aspects of those faults that continue to block the redemption of Zion.

First, there is a persistent hunger for the things of this world with its attendant selfishness and envying, against which the prophets have always spoken out in boldness. As his society turned from a righteous to a wicked nation in just a few years, Nephi wrote: "There began to be some disputings among the people; and some were lifted up unto pride and boastings because of their exceedingly great riches, yea, even unto great persecutions. . . . And the people began to be distinguished by ranks. . . . And thus there became a great inequality in all the land. . . . Now the cause of this iniquity of the people was this—Satan had great power, unto the stirring up of the people to do all manner of iniquity, and to the puffing them up with pride, tempting them to seek for power, and authority, and riches, and the vain things of the world." (3 Nephi 6:10–15.)

Lest we falsely believe that those circumstances applied uniquely to the Nephite church, it is well to keep in mind these somber words of Moroni, speaking to *our* generation and time:

"Behold, I speak unto you as if ye were present, and yet ye are not. But behold, Jesus Christ hath shown you unto me, and I know your doing.

"And I know that ye do walk in the pride of your hearts; and there are none save a few only who do not lift themselves up in the pride of their hearts, unto the wearing of very fine apparel, unto envying, and strifes, and malice, and persecutions, and all manner of iniquities; and your churches, yea, even every one, have become polluted because of the pride of your hearts.

"For behold, ye do love money, and your substance, and your fine apparel, and the adorning of your churches, more than ye love the poor and the needy, the sick and the afflicted." (Mormon 8:35–37.)

As have his fellow prophets, Brigham Young sorrowed often over the weaknesses of the Saints. Even as Johnston's Army approached in 1857, Brigham said: "I am more afraid of covetousness in our elders than I am of the hordes of hell. Have we men out now of that class? I believe so. I am afraid of such spirits; for they are more powerful and injurious to this people than all hell outside of our borders. All our enemies . . . and all hell with them marshalled against us, could not do us the injury that covetousness in the hearts of this people could do." (*Journal of Discourses,* 5:350.)

Many other quotations could be given illustrating Brigham Young's concern about the spiritual malingering of some of the Saints. One additional comment will suffice. In President Young's last sermon, he said: "The devils in hell [are] looking at this people

. . . and trying to overthrow us, and the people are still shaking hands with the servants of the devil, instead of sanctifying themselves and calling upon the Lord and doing the work which he has commanded us and put into our hands to do." (*Journal of Discourses,* 18:304.)

Secondly, Zion was not redeemed earlier in this dispensation because the Saints were not united, nor can it be until we practice the strength found in unity. "Let the Saints of the Most High ever cultivate this principle, and the most glorious blessings must result, not only to them individually, but to the whole church the order of the kingdom will be maintained, its officers respected, and its requirements readily and cheerfully obeyed." (*TPJS,* p. 174.)

Unity is one of the central themes of the gospel. In His great intercessory prayer, Jesus asked for His apostles "that they all may be one; as thou, Father, art in me, and I in thee, that they also may be one in us: that the world may believe that thou hast sent me." (John 17:21.) The people of Enoch were of one heart and one mind as were those in the golden days of the Nephite church. "If ye are not one ye are not mine." (D&C 38:27.) "And all things shall be done by common consent in the church." (D&C 26:2.)

It is self-evident that the third reason for failure to redeem Zion falls upon those who do not keep the commandments of God and who thus cannot be pure in heart. At a time when the Saints who had gathered in Missouri were suffering great persecution, the Lord revealed through the Prophet Joseph that their afflictions had come upon them "in consequence of their transgressions. . . . There were jarrings, and contentions, and envyings, and strifes, and lustful and covetous desires among them; therefore by these things they polluted their inheritances." (D&C 101:2, 6.) The Lord must have a pure people to do His work. "It takes a Zion people to make a Zion society," as President Benson has reminded us. (*Ensign,* May 1986, p. 4.)

Though the gulf between the Church and the world is wide, and becoming wider, it is well to remember this is the great day of Satan's power. He seduces many, even of the elect, lulling "them away into carnal security," and thus he "cheateth their souls, and leadeth them . . . carefully down to hell." (2 Nephi 28:21.) We lose too many to the adversary. Too many of our members are part-time disciples, trying to live with one foot in the world and the other in the kingdom. Others cringe in shame before the mocking crowds in the "great and spacious building" (1 Nephi 11:36) of the world, careless and casual in their commitment, and, like the seed that fell upon stony ground (see Matthew 13), soon wither away and are lost. Too many deny Christ as they disregard and hold up for contempt the sacred covenants made in God's holy temples.

Harsh words? Perhaps, but listen to President Spencer W. Kimball's somber warning given in an inspired message on the occasion of the bicentennial of the United States: "Carnal man has tended to transfer his trust in God to material things. . . . When men have fallen under the power of Satan, and lost the faith, they have put in its place a hope in the 'arm of flesh' and in 'gods of silver, and gold, of brass'—that is, in idols. . . . Many people spend most of their time working the service of a self-image that includes sufficient money, stocks, bonds, investment portfolios, property, credit cards, furnishings, automobiles, and the like to *guarantee* carnal security throughout, it is hoped, a long and happy life. . . . We must leave off the worship of modern-day idols and a reliance on the 'arm of flesh,' for the Lord has said to all the world in our day, 'I will not spare any that remain in Babylon.' . . . When I review the performance of this people [those in America] in comparison with what is expected, I am appalled and frightened."

Then, speaking directly to the Saints, President Kimball continued: "The Brethren constantly cry out against that which is intolerable in the sight of the Lord: against pollution of mind, body, and our surroundings; against vulgarity, stealing, lying, pride, and blasphemy; against fornication, adultery, homosexuality, and all other abuses of the sacred power to create; against murder and all that is like unto it; against all manner of desecration.

"That such a cry should be necessary among a people so blessed is amazing to me. And that such things should be found even among the Saints to some degree is scarcely believable, for these are a people who are in possession of many gifts of the Spirit, who have knowledge that puts the eternities into perspective, who have been shown the way to eternal life.

"Sadly, however, we find that to be shown the way is not necessarily to walk in it, and many have not been able to continue in faith. These have submitted themselves in one degree or another to the enticings of Satan and his servants and joined with those of 'the world' in lives of ever-deepening idolatry." (*Ensign*, June 1976, pp. 4, 6.)

President Kimball was right, of course. There is no way around it. We must do better if we are to establish Zion! President Harold B. Lee also made this point very clear: "I have had great difficulty understanding how a people who are not able to sacrifice to a point where they can pay a tenth of their interest annually . . . are more than 10% ready for the United Order." (*Conference Report,* October 1941, p. 113.)

In light of our shortcomings as individuals and as a people, how thankful I am for God's loving mercy: "Verily I say unto you, notwithstanding their [the Saints'] sins, my bowels are filled with compassion towards them. I will not utterly cast them off; and in the day of wrath I will remember mercy." (D&C 101:9.)

THE PURE IN HEART

Though Zion is a place and a people, perhaps the definition that best describes it is "the pure in heart." (D&C 97:21.) In that connection it must be noted that Zion itself is by its very nature perfect, flawless, constant in its purity and beauty, totally clean before God, without imperfections of any kind. Although the members of The Church of Jesus Christ of Latter-day Saints who live in stakes and wards are already gathered, in a sense, to a prototypical, pre-millennial Zion, that of which we are now a part is intended to prepare us for the perfect Zion to come. We are being schooled and trained for better things. We are as children learning sums before proceeding to a study of calculus, playing with blocks before building a great edifice.

An important principle of this training program is that the institution is not what makes people good; rather, it is goodness that permits the institution to be established. Zion cannot be established with impure people who have not completely consecrated their lives to Christ. Zion will be established only when the Saints are pure! When we are pure, Zion will come.

THE DREAM OF ZION

In its complete sense, then, Zion remains for us the golden, flawless ideal, the dream of what we may become if we are worthy, the goal toward which we must labor, the paradise which though now lost may yet be regained. The dream of establishing Zion thus is a dream of perfection that deals with the conquest of the heart rather than with constructing buildings or paving streets with gold. It calls us to subdue and purify our passions, to overcome the carnality of the natural man; and to become "as a child, submissive, meek, humble, patient, full of love, willing to submit to all things which the Lord seeth fit to inflict upon [us], even as a child doth submit to his father." (Mosiah 3:19.) To do so is a daunting task. Like every great journey, it commences with a single step.

Remember the journey of Zion's Camp? Various brethren were called to march from Ohio to come to the aid of Zion (Jackson County, Missouri), to bring military relief to the persecuted Saints there. But when the several hundred men who had marched from Ohio neared their intended destination, the Prophet Joseph disbanded them. Was the expedition a failure? Perhaps yes, in one sense; but from a broader point of view, a glorious victory was achieved. It was not a military victory, of course, but one of the spirit, as men learned to purify and sanctify themselves in Zion's cause. Of that march Elder Dallin H. Oaks has said: "Most of the men who were to lead the Church for the next half-century, including those who would take the Saints across the plains and colonize the Intermountain West, came to know the Prophet Joseph and received their formative leadership training in the march of Zion's Camp." (*Ensign*, November 1985, p. 62.) Elder Orson F. Whitney said of Zion's Camp: "The redemption of Zion is more than the purchase or recovery of lands, the building of cities, or even the founding of nations." (*Life of Heber C. Kimball*, 2nd ed. [Salt Lake City: Stevens and Wallis, Inc., 1945], p. 65.) At its center, the redemption of Zion is the purification of souls.

But is the establishment of Zion only a golden dream, forever unobtainable, ever receding before us like an illusion? To the Latter-day Saints, who believe in the eventual perfectibility of mankind, there *can* be a Zion on earth, as there has been already, albeit only twice, and that but briefly. We are thus under sacred obligation to awake, arise, and get to work; to make its attainment "our greatest object"; to "push many people to Zion with songs of everlasting joy upon their heads." (D&C 66:11.) There must be no sense of undue haste; the order of the kingdom must be maintained and the work done "in the Lord's way." But delay is inexcusable. As always, the greatest and most difficult task will be *to change ourselves*. "Go ye out from Babylon. Be ye clean. . . . Go ye out from among the nations, even from Babylon, from the midst of wickedness, which is spiritual Babylon." (D&C 133:5, 14.) Our greatest task, as a people and as individual Saints, is to purify ourselves, to give away all of our sins to know Christ (see Alma 22:18), to live all of Christ's commandments. That is the measure of our devotion, of our commitment to Him. In what may well be the greatest verse in all of Holy Writ, Jesus explained: "He that hath my commandments, and keepeth them, he it is that loveth me: and he that loveth me shall be loved of my Father, and I will love him, and will manifest myself to him." (John 14:21.)

Thus, "let everyone labour to prepare himself for the vineyard, sparing a little time to comfort the mourners; to bind up the broken hearted; to reclaim the backslider; to bring back the wanderer; to reinvite into the Kingdom such as have been cut off. . . . To work righteousness, and with one heart and one mind prepare to help redeem Zion, that goodly land of promise where the willing and obedient shall be blessed." (*History of the Church*, 2:229.)

Chapter Two

Becoming Pure
in Heart

Defining and describing Zion, while undoubtedly important and interesting, are not sufficient. If we accept the Prophet Joseph's dictum that building up Zion is our greatest task, then much more is required. Zion can be established only by those who are pure in heart and whose focus is on the kingdom of God rather than upon Babylon: "No man can serve two masters: for either he will hate the one, and love the other; or else he will hold to the one, and despise the other. Ye cannot serve God and mammon," said Jesus. (Matthew 6:24.) Nephi echoed that theme: "The laborer in Zion shall labor for Zion; for if they labor for money they shall perish." (2 Nephi 26:31.) Any weakening of focus or attention, any vacillating in purpose or energy, will only delay the redemption of Zion. Clean hands, pure hearts, and an eye single to the glory of God are required.

Those whose hearts are pure do the right things for the right reasons. Their motives are pure and unsullied by self-interest, ambition, pride, or malice. Hearts that are pure are broken and contrite, humble and devoid of guile. Consistent and concerted daily effort is needed to attain and maintain such Christ-like behavior. "When ye shall do your alms," said Jesus to the Nephites, "do not sound a trumpet before you, as will hypocrites do in the synagogues and in the streets, that they may have glory of men. Verily I say unto you, they have their reward." (3 Nephi 13:2.)

The great struggle of life is to overcome the natural man, with his carnality and selfishness, and to become a Saint of God through the Atonement of Christ. It is not a struggle once won forever finished, but a battle that must be engaged every day that we live. As Nephi said, "If ye shall press forward, feasting upon the word of Christ, and *endure to the end,* behold, thus saith the Father: Ye shall have eternal life." (2 Nephi 31:20; italics added.)

Whatever our age or status, we must never lower our guard or slacken our efforts. In his great valedictory sermon, King Benjamin warned, "If ye do not watch yourselves, and your thoughts, and your words, and your deeds, and observe the commandments of God, and continue in the faith of what ye have heard . . . even unto the end of your lives, ye must perish." (Mosiah 4:30.)

President John Taylor, who knew more than most about trials and tribulations, had this to say about the Latter-day Saints: "The only fear I have for the Latter-day Saints is that they will not live their religion. And I call upon you here to-day to lay aside your covetousness, your greed and your avarice, and act honorably and justly one with another as your brethren, humble yourselves before God and seek unto him for his guidance, and he will help you, he will bless and sustain you, and he will deliver you." (*Journal of Discourses,* 21:6.)

Knowing something of the amazing capacity of the human race to rationalize, to temporize, to vacillate, those who struggle to be pure in heart will constantly reexamine and critique their own motives and actions. They will wake each morning with a godly discontent in their hearts and commit themselves to action, no matter what the cost in toil and sacrifice. "Woe . . . unto him that is at ease in Zion!" (2 Nephi 28:24.)

The great prophet Alma knew the importance of self-examination: "Can ye look up to God . . . with a pure heart and clean hands . . . having the image of God engraven upon your countenances? . . . If ye have experienced a change of heart, and if ye have felt to sing the song of redeeming love, . . . can ye feel so now? Have ye walked, keeping yourselves blameless before God? Could ye say, if ye were called to die at this time, . . . that ye have been sufficiently humble? . . . Are ye stripped of pride? . . . Is there one among you who is not stripped of envy? . . . Is there one among you that doth make a mock of his brother, or that heapeth upon him persecutions?" (Alma 5:19, 26–30.) Our answers to those and similar questions tell much about our motives and the desires of our hearts.

COME UNTO CHRIST

Those who are pure in heart focus their lives on the Father and Son. They have an eye single to the glory of God. They seek to "come unto Christ, . . . and partake of his salvation, and the power of his redemption." They strive to "offer [their] whole souls as an offering unto him." (Omni 1:26.)

What does it mean to come unto Christ? How does it change our lives? The answers are both simple and profound. They include the following:

1. *To come unto Christ is to partake of His glorious atonement.* In a sense the atonement is free—or at least part of it is. The Christ who died on Calvary's cross and rose again the third day—the Christ of the empty tomb—purchased immortality for all of us with His blood. We need not come to Him to enjoy *that* blessing. He gives it to us, at no cost, with no effort on our part. It is His gift to all, the

"grace that so fully he proffers [us]." (*Hymns,* no. 193.) But the second phase, if you will, of the Atonement, the gift of eternal life with the Father and Son—though it can never be fully earned—must at least be worked for. Jesus promises that if we exercise faith in Him and repent of our sins and shortcomings, His infinite grace will make up the deficit between our shortcomings and what is needed to render us worthy to return to our Father's house. He pleads with us to repent of our sins, forsake them, and come unto Him. Then, and only then, can He bear the burdens of our sins. Only then can they be washed away by His atoning blood. "For behold, I, God, have suffered these things for all, that they might not suffer if they would repent; but if they would not repent, they must suffer even as I." (D&C 19:16–17; see also 2 Nephi 2:7, Mosiah 3:12.)

No mortal being fully lives the celestial life. Each falls short of fully and perfectly keeping all of the commandments. Perfection in every aspect of life eludes us. How easy it is to get discouraged, to say, "I know the gospel's true; I just can't live it. I'm just not strong enough." The glory of the Atonement is that Jesus makes up the deficit in our performance if we truly repent. He asks that we do our very best, holding nothing back, doing all that we can. Unfortunately, we do not always do so. That is where He steps in. His perfection and grace will save the repentant sinner from the imperfection that is part of the human condition. Joseph Smith saw in vision those in the celestial kingdom: "Just [souls] made perfect through Jesus the mediator of the new covenant, who wrought out this perfect atonement through the shedding of his own blood." (D&C 76:69.)

Elder Bruce R. McConkie's paean of praise to the Christ whom he loved reads in part: "I believe in Christ, he ransoms me./From Satan's grasp he sets me free, . . . /And while I strive through grief and pain,/His voice is heard: 'ye shall obtain.'" (*Hymns,* no. 134.) Faithful trust in Christ's redeeming love and grace, while going forward, "in grief and pain" if need be, will move us toward our celestial goal.

We often seem unwilling to take Christ at His word, to *really*, in our heart of hearts, believe Him when He says, "Come unto me." We hold back, embarrassed by our own imperfections, convinced we just can't do what is needed, filled with guilt, self-doubt, and even perhaps despair. To such Jesus says, from the fullness and perfection of His love: "Come unto me, all ye that labour and are heavy laden, and I will give you rest. Take my yoke upon you, and learn of me; for I am meek and lowly in heart: and ye shall find rest unto your souls. For my yoke is easy, and my burden is light." (Matthew 11:28–30.) His love is sufficient to sustain us in our weakness. He stands ready to "encircle [us] in the arms of [His] safety." (Alma 34:16.) Oh, how He longs to come into our lives if we will but let Him do so!

In John's revelation we hear the gentle pleading of the Savior: "Behold, I stand at the door, and knock: if any man hear my voice, and open the door, I will come in to him, and will sup with him, and he with me." (Revelation 3:20.) Note the need for more than good intentions on our part; action also is required. Coming to Christ requires that *we* move.

2. *To come to Christ is to acknowledge Him as Lord and Master.* We are His servants, blessed to be His undershepherds. To all who labor in His service, He calls, "Feed my lambs . . . feed my sheep." (John 21:15–17.) The day must surely come—I testify that it will—when each of us will report his or her stewardship to the Judge and King of all. That report will be given on our knees!

If Christ be our Lord and Master, and we His servant children, our greatest wish will be to be obedient to His commandments. It is an obedience born of love, not fear, not given begrudgingly or half-heartedly but freely, voluntarily. A beloved old Mormon hymn, author unknown, reminds us that although God will plead and persuade, He will not force us to heaven. (See *Hymns,* no. 240.) His very nature forbids it. A war was fought in heaven to uphold that principle. As we accept Christ as Lord and Master, "we talk of [Him], we rejoice in [Him], we preach of [Him], we prophesy of [Him], and we write according to our prophecies, that our children may know to what source they may look for a remission of their sins." (2 Nephi 25:26.)

These words by the great English hymn writer Isaac Watts express well the feelings of humble gratitude and renewed resolution that flood our souls as we contemplate the true place of Christ in our lives and acknowledge Him as the fount of all blessings:

> When I survey the wondrous cross,
> On which the Prince of glory died,
> My richest gain I count but loss,
> And pour contempt on all my pride.
> Were the whole realm of nature mine,
> That were a present far too small;
> Love so amazing, so divine,
> Demands my soul, my life, my all.
> (*Westminster Choir College Library* [Bryn
> Mawr, Penn.: Theodore Presser Co., 1970].)

3. *To come to Christ is to learn the equality of heaven.* With the Father and Son there is no privilege of rank or position—no keys of secular or ecclesiastical title, heritage, or influence that unlock heaven's door. God is not concerned about or influenced by race, gender, or social status. He to whom all are alike (see 2 Nephi 26:33; Acts 17:26) invites *all* to come unto Him. Whether people are rich or poor has little to do, in and of itself, with whether they are wicked or righteous. Although in a general way the cross of gold is harder to bear than that of poverty (see Matthew 19:23–24), both affluence and penury can be trials of the soul.

Jesus spoke out against the rich who will not give their substance to the poor as well as against the poor whose hearts are not broken, and He found fault with both. (See D&C 56:16–17.) The poor who are "pure in heart," however, "whose hearts are broken, and whose spirits are contrite, . . . shall see the kingdom of God coming in power and great glory unto their deliverance; for the fatness of the earth shall be theirs." (D&C 56:18.)

Racism—the abominable doctrine that claims superiority of one person over another by reason of race, ethnicity, or cultural background—remains as one of the abiding tragedies of societies the world over. The cause of much of the strife and conflict in the world, it is an offense against God and a tool in the devil's hands. Jesus always acted toward others in ways that underlined their worth as human beings, regardless of background or past actions. He received sinners and ate with them, reminding the self-righteous that there is more joy in heaven over "one sinner that repenteth . . . than over ninety and nine just persons, which need no repentance." (Luke 15:7.) God's modern-day prophets have spoken out on the subject of prejudice and bigotry in plain and unmistakable language: "We repudiate efforts to deny to any person his or her inalienable dignity and rights on the abhorrent and tragic theory of the superiority of one race or color over another." (Statement of the First Presidency, December 3, 1987.)

To come to Christ is to be "color-blind," to see all men and women everywhere as one's brothers and sisters. Little children have that ability, as the following sweet letter received from a young African-American girl living in the Birmingham Alabama 3rd Ward attests:

> For my birthday I had a sleep-over party. I invited two good friends of mine from class, Nicole who is black and Cameron who

is white. Nicole asked me why I invited Cameron and I told her
that Cameron is one of my best friends and I wanted her to be
there for my birthday. But Nicole said black and white shouldn't
mix if they don't have to.

That night I told Mommy what Nicole said and she said to me
that if we can't learn to get along, and live together, how can we
expect to return to live with Heavenly Father? And I told Nicole
that the next day, but I didn't know if she would come to my party.
She did, and we all had a good time. It was a great party. I remember learning in Primary that we are all children of God, and we
should act that way. I have a testimony that I am a child of God.
In the name of Jesus Christ. Amen.

Zandra Stovall, September 22, 1991

4. *To come to Christ leads us to joy.* Significantly, the angel who
announced to frightened shepherds the birth of Jesus said to them,
"Fear not: for, behold, I bring you good tidings of great joy, which
shall be unto all people." (Luke 2:10.) The psalmist sang, "My soul
shall be joyful in the Lord." (Psalm 35:9.) Joy should not be con-
fused with pleasure, though it often is. Pleasure, the opposite of pain,
is of the senses. It is by its very nature fleeting, short-lived, needing
constant reinforcement. Seeking it leads too often to self-indulgence,
selfishness, and moral slackness. Pleasure "pulls no handcarts." Joy,
on the other hand, is of the Spirit. It may co-exist with suffering and
sacrifice. It transcends the body. One can be "joyful in all our tribu-
lation." (2 Corinthians 7:4.)

Joy is more profound than is pleasure. Ammon, the great
Nephite missionary, was so "swallowed up in the joy of his God"
that he fell exhausted to the earth. (See Alma 27:17.) Unlike pleasure, joy is not self-centered. Alma's joy was "more full because of
the success of [his] brethren," and when he thought of their success,
his soul was "carried away, even to the separation of it from the
body, as it were, so great [was his] joy." (Alma 29:14, 16.)

Christ's redeeming sacrifice provides for us the ultimate joy, that of coming to a world of spiritual testing and moral agency, with the promise that if we are true and faithful, enduring to the end, we may return to dwell evermore in the presence of the Father and Son. Thus, the faithful who look forward to Christ's coming, who suffer "all manner of afflictions, for [His] sake," are "filled with great joy because of the resurrection of the dead, according to the will and power and deliverance of Jesus Christ from the bands of death." (Alma 4:3–14.)

Indeed, Christ is the way, the truth, the life, and the light. To come to Him in faith and joy, leaving behind the sins and prejudices of this world and of the natural man, His avowed enemy, should be our goal. Those who do so pray they might be found worthy, after this mortal probation comes to a close, to inherit the mansions prepared for them in our Father's kingdom.

PROVIDE SERVICE

For many, Christ is found through righteous service to others. Service is the key that unlocks the doors to celestial halls.

What is there about service that purifies hearts and brings souls to Christ? There is no single answer but rather several. Service drives out selfishness, the great enemy of spirituality. The "natural man," carnal, sensual, and devilish, is deeply selfish, caring not for the unfortunate, not interested in helping to meet the needs of others. He sees them only as creatures to be used to gratify *his* wants and then to be thrown away. His ears are stopped up against the pleas of the oppressed, the poor, those in pain. Their cries of suffering are of no consequence or interest to him.

Service helps us develop compassion, that most Christ-like of virtues. Compassion is more than sympathy. It involves empathy—

an ability to feel deeply the pain of others as though we were one
with them. "Are we not all beggars?" asked compassionate King
Benjamin. "Do we not all depend upon the same Being, even God,
for all the substance which we have, for both food and raiment, and
for gold, and for silver, and for all the riches which we have of every
kind?" (Mosiah 4:19.) Compassion goes beyond empathy to action,
impelling us to bind up the wounds, "succor the weak, lift up the
hands which hang down, and strengthen the feeble knees" (D&C
81:5) of those less fortunate than ourselves. It was of the compassionate that Christ spoke when He said, "Come, ye blessed of my
Father, inherit the kingdom prepared for you from the foundation of
the world: for I was an hungered, and ye gave me meat: I was thirsty,
and ye gave me drink: I was a stranger, and ye took me in: naked,
and ye clothed me: I was sick, and ye visited me: I was in prison, and
ye came unto me.

"Then shall the righteous answer him, saying, Lord, when saw
we thee an hungered, and fed thee? or thirsty, and gave thee drink?
When saw we thee a stranger, and took thee in? or naked, and
clothed thee? Or when saw we thee sick, or in prison, and came unto
thee?

"And the King shall answer and say unto them, Verily I say unto
you, Inasmuch as ye have done it unto one of the least of these my
brethren, ye have done it unto me." (Matthew 25:34–40.)

As we develop compassion, the scales of indifference, self-right-
eousness, and selfishness fall from our eyes. We see and feel—perhaps for the first time—the suffering of others. We weep with them
and for them. We weep, too, for our own weaknesses and imperfections. We reach out to help the less fortunate as best we can. We
think less of ourselves and more of others. We set different priori-
ties, eschewing the tawdry materialism that has claimed so much of
our attention heretofore. We set aside "our consuming selfishness,"

our "love for comfort and ease" (see President Gordon B. Hinckley, *Ensign*, November 1991, p. 52) and seek to aid those less fortunate than ourselves.

There is so much of suffering in the world, so much of selfishness and indifference, too few tears for those whose burdens are heavy, too little heartfelt concern for others. How easy it is to switch off the television set rather than be haunted by the faces of hollow-eyed children in Africa or of frightened refugees in a dozen places with strange-sounding names. Their sorrow and want make us uneasy. They prick our hearts and arouse our slumbering consciences, and too often we tune them out rather than bear their sorrows. They remind us of neglected responsibilities. Perhaps our response may be, "The man has brought upon himself his misery; therefore I will stay my hand, and will not give unto him of my food, nor impart unto him of my substance that he may not suffer, for his punishments are just." Unto such comes this inspired reply: "Whosoever doeth this . . . hath great cause to repent; and except he repenteth of that which he hath done he perisheth forever, and hath no interest in the kingdom of God. . . . For the sake of retaining a remission of your sins from day to day, that ye may walk guiltless before God—I would that ye should impart of your substance to the poor, every man according to that which he hath." (Mosiah 4:17–18, 26.)

We lighten Christ's yoke as we accept some of the burdens of others, as we help them to have hope rather than dark despair, as we apply a healing balm of Gilead to their scarified, suffering souls.

A recent issue of the *Wall Street Journal* (November 13, 1992, pp. A1, A16) recounted a heartwarming tale of suffering, compassion, and Christ-like service. Some fifteen years ago, Dr. Ian Jackson, a world-famous craniofacial surgeon, was on a charity mission from his native Scotland to Peru. There he met David Lopez, a tiny Indian boy, just two years old, who had virtually no face at all. A gaping hole covered the areas where his mouth and nose should have been. There were no upper teeth or upper jaw. To drink, David simply tilted back his head and poured the liquid straight down. His lower teeth could actually touch his forehead. Most of David's face had literally been eaten away by a terrible parasitic disease called leishmaniasis.

Relief workers begged Dr. Jackson to help. He was leaving for Scotland the next day but agreed to try to rebuild David's face if the boy could come to Scotland. Eventually, a way was found, and the Jacksons went to Glasgow Airport to pick up David. As he walked down the ramp, they saw a tiny boy wearing scuffed white boots and a hand-knit poncho. A woolen cap was pulled so low on his head that only his big brown eyes and the round hole beneath them were visible.

The Jacksons took David into their home and into their hearts. There followed long years of surgery—more than eighty operations in all—as Dr. Jackson attempted to give David a new face. All of the doctor's services were donated. Each summer, as other children played, David was in the hospital, his head swathed in bandages.

The painstaking, pioneering surgical efforts to rebuild David's face have gone on for fifteen years. Today, David looks like a young man who has been in a serious automobile accident, but he is well-adjusted and fully functional. He used to be teased and tormented about his looks, but over the years that has died away.

The Jacksons now live in the United States, where Dr. Jackson continues to be one of the leading craniofacial surgeons in the world. In 1982, Mrs. Jackson flew to Peru to try to find David's parents. After a long journey down-river from a remote Catholic mission, David's father was found. He explained that the boy had been born healthy but when he developed leishmaniasis after having been bitten by an infected sandfly, he was taken to the mission to seek treatment. The father gave permission to the Jacksons—who had developed a deep love for David—to adopt him as their own. Since 1984, David Lopez has been David Jackson. Now in his senior year of high school in Michigan, David is a top soccer player and competes on the school wrestling team, though his mother cringes every time his reconstructed face slams into the mat.

I don't know whether Dr. Jackson is a Christian or not, but I do know he is doing God's work. "When ye are in the service of your fellow beings ye are only in the service of your God." (Mosiah 2:17.) "If I had a hero," David says, "it would be my dad."

As we lose our lives in compassionate service to others, we develop a deeper understanding of our dependence on God. I return again to the wisdom of King Benjamin: "And now, if God, who has created you, on whom you are dependent for your lives and for all that ye have and are, doth grant unto you whatsoever ye ask that is right, in faith, believing that ye shall receive, O then, how ye ought to impart of the substance that ye have one to another." (Mosiah 4:21.) Said faithful Nephi, "I know in whom I have trusted. My God hath been my support; he hath led me through afflictions in the wilderness; and he hath preserved me upon the waters of the great deep. He hath filled me with his love, even unto the consuming of my flesh. He hath heard my cry by day, and he hath given me knowledge by visions in the nighttime. And upon the wings of his Spirit hath my body been carried away. . . . I will trust in him forever." (2 Nephi 4:19–25, 34.)

A decision to serve God through serving others leads faithful priesthood bearers to bless the sick. As the faith of those who bless unites with that of the recipient of the blessing, great miracles can and do occur. That principle is well illustrated by an event of great importance in the history of the Church in eastern North Carolina as described by Joel Grant Hancock in *Strengthened by the Storm: The Coming of the Mormons to Harkers Island, North Carolina, 1897–1909* (Morehead City, North Carolina: Campbell and Campbell, 1988).

In the late 1890s, Joseph Wallace Willis, his wife Margaret, and their numerous children lived in a little community called Diamond City, located on one of the Outer Banks of North Carolina. The people of Diamond City, most of them fishermen and on-shore whalers, were poor and humble but full of faith. One of the Willis children was a twelve-year-old girl named Bertha. She was chronically ill with rheumatoid arthritis, bedridden for days at a time, her only diversion reading from the large family Bible. "Because her hands were swollen shut by the crippling disease, she would resort to opening the book with her elbows and would then read it at whatever point it might fall open." (P. 42.) On January 8, 1898, as Bertha struggled to read the scriptures, the book fell open to James 5:14–15: "Is any sick among you? let him call for the elders of the church; and let them pray over him, anointing him with oil in the name of the Lord: And the prayer of faith shall save the sick, and the Lord shall raise him up."

From her bedroom window Bertha had watched two visitors to her little community. They were Mormon elders—the first in the area—Elders John Witt Telford of Bountiful, Utah, and William Hansen of Logan, Utah. Bertha had heard these two young men referred to as "elders" and knew of no others who answered to that title. "Perhaps," she thought, "they are the men referred to in the Bible." With the faith of a child, she spoke to her mother about it. "Mama," she said, "I believe those Mormon elders could heal me."

"I guess they could, if you have the faith," her mother replied. (Ibid.)

Soon the missionaries were sent for, and they gave Bertha a

priesthood blessing. Several hours later, after they had gone, Bertha called to her mother in the adjoining room. "Mama, Mama, come look," she exclaimed. "My fingers, they are limber! I can open and shut my hands." The next morning her parents "were awakened by the sound of their daughter preparing breakfast in the kitchen. It was the first time she had walked unassisted for months." (Ibid., p. 43.)

The entire family of Joseph Wallace Willis eventually joined the Church, most on Harkers Island, a few miles from Shackleford Banks, on which Diamond City was located. At a family reunion in 1986, more than 250 direct descendants of Joseph Willis were counted as members of the Church.

Bertha, the girl healed through the administration of Elders Telford and Hansen, has a grandson, Joel Grant Hancock, a counselor in the Kinston North Carolina stake presidency (as of May 1992), who wrote the book from which this account was taken.

Human history is full of inspiring examples of the willingness of some to serve others, often at great personal danger. The following story illustrates the principle.

On December 11–13, 1862, a great Union army, commanded by General Ambrose Burnside, first bombarded and then temporarily occupied the town of Fredericksburg, Virginia. The attack was seen rather fancifully by Union generals as a prelude to a hoped-for victorious march toward Richmond, the Confederate capital. After fierce house-to-house fighting and heavy losses, the Federals were finally able to occupy the ruined town.

They then turned their attention to Marye's Heights, a large hill overlooking the town, where 6,000 Rebels awaited them under the superb command of a military genius, Robert E. Lee. The ensuing battle proved to be one of Lee's greatest military triumphs. The Southern troops were in secure defensive positions behind a stone wall that meandered along the foot of the hill. In addition, they stood four deep on a sunken road behind the wall, out of sight of Union forces.

The Union troops—more than 40,000 strong—launched a series of suicidal attacks across open ground, which stretched steadily upward for more than half a mile from the Rappahannock River toward Marye's Heights. They were met by withering blasts of musket fire from the Confederate positions, and by deadly artillery fire from guns on Marye's Heights. Mowed down by a scythe of shot, none got closer than forty yards from the stone wall.

Soon the ground in front of the Confederate positions was littered with hundreds—then thousands—of blue uniforms, more than twelve thousand before sunset on Saturday, December 13. Crying for help, the wounded lay in the bitter cold throughout that terrible night. Hundreds died from their wounds and from exposure.

The next day, a Sunday, dawned cold and foggy. As the morning fog lifted, the agonized cries of the wounded could still be heard. Finally, a young Confederate soldier, a nineteen-year-old sergeant from G Company, Second South Carolina Regiment, had taken all he could stand. The young man's name was Richard Rowland Kirkland. To his commanding officer, Kirkland exclaimed, "All night and all day I have heard those poor people crying for water, and I can stand it no longer. I . . . ask permission to go and give them water." His request was initially denied on the grounds that it was too dangerous. Finally, however, permission was granted, and thousands of amazed men on both sides saw the young soldier, with several canteens draped around his neck, climb over the wall and walk to the nearest wounded Union soldier. He raised the stricken man's head, gently gave him a drink, and covered him with his own overcoat. Then he moved to the next of the wounded and the next and the next.

As Kirkland's purpose became clear, fresh cries of "Water, water, for God's sake, water" arose all over the field.

The Federal soldiers were at first too surprised to shoot. Soon they began to cheer the young Southerner as they saw what he was doing. For more than an hour and a half, Sergeant Kirkland continued his work of mercy.

Tragically, Richard Kirkland was himself killed a few months later at the battle of Chicamauga. His last words to his companions were, "Save yourselves and tell my Pa I died right."

Kirkland's Christ-like compassion made his name synonymous with mercy for a post-Civil War generation, both North and South. He became known by soldiers on both sides of the conflict as "the angel of Marye's Heights." His loving errand of mercy is commemorated by a bronze monument that stands today in front of the stone wall at Fredericksburg. It was crafted by Felix De Weldon, who also sculpted the Iwo Jima monument, in Washington, D.C. The statue depicts Sergeant Kirkland lifting the head of a wounded Union soldier to give him a drink of refreshing water. A tablet hangs in Kirkland's honor in the Episcopal church in Gettysburg. With simple eloquence it captures the essence of the young soldier's Christ-like mission of mercy. It reads, "A hero of benevolence, at the risk of his own life, he gave his enemy drink at Fredericksburg." (See *The Battle of Fredericksburg* [Philadelphia: Eastern Acorn Press, 1990]; "He Gave His Enemy Drink," *CWT Illustrated,* October 1962, pp. 38–39; information on Richard Kirkland provided by the staff of the Fredericksburg and Spotsylvania National Military Park, National Park Service, U.S. Department of the Interior.)

Sergeant Kirkland's act of mercy touches all hearts. It reminds us, in dramatic fashion, of the heights to which the human spirit can soar. What a strange creature is man! Capable of the most grievous sins, of cruelty and evil almost unbelievable in their horror, he also rises to heights of sublime love and compassion for others. The forces of evil struggle with those of good in every human breast, yet even in the midst of the blood and horror of war there remain some whose hearts are touched by the Spirit of Christ, who refuse to become "without affection . . . [hating] their own blood." (See Moses 7:33.)

So it was in the last days of the Nephites, when nearly "every heart was hardened, so that they delighted in the shedding of blood continually." (Mormon 4:11.) Though he knew that the judgments of the Lord would fall upon his people, the great prophet-soldier Mormon led them in battle, "notwithstanding their wickedness," because he "loved them, according to the love of God which was in [him], with all [his] heart." (Mormon 3:12.) In every major human conflict there are those who rise above blood and horror to the broad sunny uplands of compassion and benevolence. Mormon was such a man, but so, too, in his own way, was Richard Kirkland, a young soldier from rural South Carolina.

WORK TOGETHER IN HARMONY AND UNITY

Among the Saints in Zion, if hearts are to be purified, there must be unanimity in decisions and unity in actions. The Lord pled with the Saints to "let every man esteem his brother as himself" (D&C 38:24) and concluded his instructions on unity with these words: "If ye are not one ye are not mine" (D&C 38:27). In Zion there is no bickering, no backbiting, but rather a spirit of oneness and cooperation, of working together for a great common cause. The Prophet Joseph explained: "The greatest temporal and spiritual blessings which always come from faithfulness and concerted effort, never attended individual exertion or enterprise. The history of all past ages abundantly attests this fact." (*TPJS,* p. 183.)

Though we have admittedly fallen short of a celestial ideal, the Saints have accomplished much through cooperative effort. Perhaps the essential value of cooperation is nowhere better illustrated than in the story of the Hole-in-the Rock expedition of 1879–1880. No pioneer company ever built a wagon road through wilder, rougher, more inhospitable country than did those intrepid men, women, and children who were called to colonize San Juan County in southeastern Utah.

The main obstacle in the two-hundred-mile trek was the Colorado River and the incredibly broken-up, almost impassable country to the east of it—country that was "nothing in the world but rock and holes, hills and hollows." (David E. Miller, *Hole in the Rock: An Epic in the Colonization of the Great American West* [Salt Lake City: University of Utah Press, 1966,] p. 119.)

Preliminary scouting reports mentioned a narrow slit in the canyon wall west of the river and suggested that a passable road could be built from that "Hole-in-the-Rock" down to the Colorado. By the time more extensive reconnaissance had been carried out, the pioneer company—some two hundred fifty men, women, and children; eighty wagons; and hundreds of loose cattle and horses—was well on its way. Although the detailed scouting reports convinced most that the proposed route was impassable, it was too late to turn back.

It took six weeks of prodigious, united effort to construct three-quarters of a mile of what passed for a road from the plateau west of the Colorado down to the river through the Hole-in-the-Rock. The work of getting the wagons down through the narrow defile was especially arduous. It required courage, daring, and total unity of effort. Each wagon, with the hind wheels rough-locked, was driven down the narrow defile with horses or oxen hitched to the front, a driver in the wagon, and as many men as could find footing hanging

on to ropes or chains attached to the rear axle to help slow the wagon
as it plummeted down the abyss. Sometimes a horse or mule was
hitched behind to slow the wagon's descent, but the unfortunate animal usually lost its footing and was dragged down the steep, bumpy
grade. The steepest part of the incline dropped 50 feet for every 100
feet forward. It is a wonder that anyone, man or beast, survived; but
miraculously all did. One who took the trip recorded the event as follows:

> The first forty feet down the wagons stood so straight in the air
> it was no desirable place to ride and the channel was so narrow the
> barrels had to be removed from the sides of the wagon in order to
> let the wagon pass through. It had to be rough locked on both hind
> wheels and then a heavy rope attached behind to which about eight
> men held back as hard as they could to keep the wagon from mak-
> ing a dash down the forty feet. The women and children took hold
> of hands and slid down this forty feet as they couldn't walk."
> (Ibid., p. 116.)

Recent events have shown that the Saints still possess and practice a high degree of cooperation and united effort. Early on Monday
morning, August 24, 1992, Hurricane Andrew reached landfall on
the South Florida coast approximately twenty-five miles south of
Miami. The storm is reported to have been the single greatest natural
disaster ever to occur in the history of the United States, with dam-
ages from its passage projected to reach $30 billion. Eighty thousand
homes were destroyed. One in every twelve families in Dade County
lost its home, and more than a hundred fifty thousand people were
left homeless. Miraculously, and through Divine Providence, not one
Church member's life was lost.

As the winds died down, the Saints promptly went to work. The
first relief and repair crews were sent out within hours of the hurricane's passage. By Thursday, August 27, all 178 salvageable mem-

bers' homes damaged by Hurricane Andrew had been temporarily repaired by volunteer work crews of local members. The Saints then expanded their efforts to help the entire community. On Saturday, August 29, more than eighteen hundred Mormon volunteers from all over the South arrived in South Florida to assist hurricane victims. The following weekend, a three-day national holiday weekend, more than fifty-one hundred LDS volunteers, working closely with units of the U.S. Army, continued to repair damaged homes, schools, and churches and to provide other community assistance. Approximately three thousand nonmembers' homes received temporary roofs, and fourteen semi-trailer loads of food, water, and medical supplies were distributed. More than twenty-one hundred dump-truck loads of debris were removed.

Many spiritually uplifting stories resulted from the heroic efforts of the clean-up volunteers. Sister Madsen, wife of Michael Madsen, president of the South Miami Florida Stake, sent the following story in a letter:

> Her name was Mrs. Greenberg, I don't know her first name. The workers went to her home. This was Saturday night, the 5th of September. There were 1800 volunteer workers. They went out from the Kendall chapel. I had a crew of about 40 workers. I was sort of their guide. They roofed about 7 homes in my area. To find more work they went across the street. I had gone up to the church to get some more supplies. When I got back, they had started to clear some debris, from about 107 St. I introduced myself to a lady standing out in front, Mrs. Greenberg. I asked her if the Mormon Elders could help her out, by clearing away some of her debris and patching her roof.
>
> She literally broke down and cried. She said this is the first time that anyone had shown that they cared. That she didn't know what to do. The men had heavy plastic and some plywood. By the time they left, it began to look like a home again. When they were through, she got her checkbook out and wanted to pay them. They

told her, this was their way of showing their gratitude. That they were representing the Latter-day Saint Church. She broke down and cried again.

Later, my husband and I went to visit her, and see how she was getting along. She said her home was liveable now. She praised the Mormon elders, and expressed her gratitude.

A brother from St. Anthony, Idaho, and other leaders from his area saw the television reports of the terrible devastation suffered by the people of South Florida. They felt a compelling need to do something to help those who had been stricken. A decision was soon made to send an eighteen-wheeler filled with Idaho potatoes to Florida. The truck was loaded with boxes and sacks of potatoes and moved swiftly across the country to the site of the disaster.

The potatoes arrived at the Kendall Chapel in the South Miami Stake in excellent condition. There was some concern that the heat and humidity would cause the potatoes to spoil. However, these fears were soon dispelled. It was amazing how welcome the potatoes were to the people of South Florida. They were so tired of eating fast foods that the potatoes were almost like a dessert.

In less than three days, all of the potatoes were distributed to needy members and nonmembers alike, as well as being made available to a local homeless shelter.

As one of the work crews was repairing a member's home, they seemed very happy and vigorous in their approach to the work. A neighbor came over and asked the member how much this crew was costing her. The member sister said: "Oh, nothing! These are members of our Mormon Church who have come here to help me. They are doing this free." The neighbor woman exclaimed, "I have two men working on my roof who are charging me $400 an hour!" The sister responded: "I think our brethren would be willing to repair your roof. Let me ask them and see." She asked the leader of the work crew if they would assist the neighbor, and the response was, "Of course, we'd be glad to help." The neighbor immediately fired the two fellows working on her roof, and it was repaired by our work crew at no expense to her. What great good was done through just a passing conversation over the fence!

"BE YE CLEAN"

Wise King Benjamin proclaimed, "I cannot tell you all the things whereby ye may commit sin; for there are divers ways and means, even so many that I cannot number them." (Mosiah 4:29.) In that spirit, I make no attempt, under the general rubric of "Be ye clean" (see Isaiah 52:11), to present a full edition of the long, lamentable catalog of human vice. I wish, however, to mention one of the most pervasive sins that blocks progress toward becoming pure in heart. It is the sin of sexual impurity, which stains and corrodes our society and blights and destroys the lives of millions.

In a momentous general conference address, President Ezra Taft Benson stated, "The plaguing sin of this generation is sexual immorality." (*Ensign,* May 1986, p. 4.) He noted that the Prophet Joseph said sexual impurity would be the source of more temptations, more buffetings, and more difficulties for the elders of Israel than any other." (*Journal of Discourses,* 8:55.) And so it is!

In his time, each of the prophets has thundered against the stain of sexual impurity. From Sinai these words rang out: "Thou shalt not commit adultery." (Exodus 20:14.) Alma said to his wayward son Corianton, "I would that ye should repent and forsake your sins, and go no more after the lusts of your eyes . . . for except ye do this ye can in nowise inherit the kingdom of God." (Alma 39:9.) President Joseph F. Smith testified, "There are at least three dangers that threaten the Church within, and the authorities need to awaken to the fact that the people should be warned unceasingly against them. As I see these, they are flattery of prominent men in the world, false educational ideas, and sexual impurity. But the third subject mentioned—personal purity, is perhaps of greater importance than either of the other two. If purity of life is neglected, all other dangers set in upon us like the rivers of waters when the flood gates are opened." (*Gospel Doctrine* [Salt Lake City: Deseret Book Company, 1986], pp. 312–13.) I shudder to think of what President Smith would think of our sex-sodden society of the late twentieth century, which knows no standards and portrays every sexual sin not only as natural but as desirable. Ours is a society that mocks at sexual purity and feeds on vice. The electronic media, with its immense ability to influence human behavior, is perhaps particularly to blame. President Thomas S. Monson noted recently that society sends adolescents a mixed message: "Advertisements and the mass media convey very heavy messages that sexual activity is acceptable and expected, inducements that sometimes drown out the warnings of experts and the pleas of parents. The Lord cuts through all the media messages with clear and precise language when He declares to us, 'Be . . . clean' (3 Nephi 20:41)." (*Ensign,* November 1990, p. 47.)

The motives behind much of the Satan-inspired plague of sexual immorality that swirls around us are clear. Those who produce and purvey smut are driven, in large part at least, by greed for money. Paul's prescient words come to mind: "The love of money is the root of all evil." (1 Timothy 6:10.) Pornography in its various forms, and I include material seen by millions on national television, yields untold millions of dollars in profit. President Gordon B. Hinckley spoke a few years ago about those who, "through the medium of [so-called] entertainment, influence or perhaps seduce millions to accept standards which are diametrically opposed to the standards of the gospel. (See *Ensign,* November 1983, pp. 45–46.)

He quoted a column written by the religion editor for the *Los Angeles Times,* which reads in part as follows:

> A survey of influential television writers and executives in Hollywood has shown that they are far less religious than the general public and diverge sharply from traditional values on such issues as abortion, homosexual rights and extramarital sex. . . . While nearly all of the 104 Hollywood professionals interviewed had a religious background, 45 percent now say they have no religion, and of the other 55 percent only 7 percent say they attend a religious service as much as once a month.
>
> This group has had a major role in shaping the shows whose themes and stars have become staples in our popular culture. . . .
>
> Eighty percent of the respondents said they did not regard homosexual relations as wrong, and 51 percent did not deem adultery as wrong. Of the 49 percent who called extramarital affairs wrong, only 17 percent felt that way strongly, the study said. Nearly all—97 percent—favored the right of a woman to choose an abortion, 91 percent holding that view strongly.
>
> By contrast, other surveys have indicated that 85 percent of Americans consider adultery wrong, 71 percent regard homosexual activity wrong, and nearly three-fourths of the public wants abortion limited to certain hard cases or banned altogether. (*Los Angeles Times*, February 19, 1983, part 2, p. 5.)

History teaches that societies that do not learn to bank and control the fires of sexual force will soon be destroyed. Ours is well on the way! Ours are the days when men call "evil good, and good evil" (Isaiah 5:20), the days when Satan "flattereth [others] away, and telleth them there is no hell; and he saith unto them: I am no devil, for there is none—and thus he whispereth in their ears, until he grasps them with his awful chains" (2 Nephi 28:22).

Those who long for a pure heart and are appalled by the "gross darkness [which covereth] the minds of the people" (D&C 112:23) clutch to their bosoms these words of Isaiah: "Depart ye, depart ye, go ye out from thence, touch no unclean thing; go ye out of the midst of her; be ye clean, that bear the vessels of the Lord" (Isaiah 52:11).

SEEK TO BRING THE CHURCH OUT OF OBSCURITY AND OUT OF DARKNESS

In my office, sitting on a finely made stand, is a large copy of Webster's *New International Dictionary,* made the more valuable to me by reason of the inscription on the flyleaf: "From President Lee's office to President Romney's office." I had occasion recently to consult the dictionary for a definition of the word *obscurity,* which I noted is "the quality or state of being obscure." Not very helpful, that. Undeterred, I then looked up the meaning of the adjective *obscure.* Of the four definitions given, three refer directly to darkness, and the fourth says, "Not noticeable, inconspicuous." Those definitions help us better understand this well-known verse from section 1 of the Doctrine & Covenants, the Lord's preface to that volume of sacred scripture: "And also those to whom these commandments were given, might have power to lay the foundation of this church, and to bring it forth out of obscurity and out of darkness, the only true and living church upon the face of the whole earth." (V. 30.)

Within the context of becoming pure in heart, it is instructive to consider in some detail each of the dictionary definitions of *obscurity.* First, obscurity in the sense of being inconspicuous, little noticed, unknown by many. Is it possible, more than one hundred sixty years after it was founded, that The Church of Jesus Christ of Latter-day Saints, "the only true and living church upon the face of the whole earth" (D&C 1:30), remains largely unknown by great numbers of people? Is it possible that might be true even here in America, the nation where the Church was founded? Despite our magnificent missionary program; despite the fact that news about the Church is avidly snatched up by the news media; despite the best efforts of our professional detractors, who do all they can to depict us as rogues and rascals, the facts seem clear.

Large numbers of Americans know almost nothing about the Church, and much of what they think they know is wrong. Bringing the Church forth out of obscurity is a task not yet completed. Indeed, it has hardly begun!

Joseph Smith, the great prophet of the Restoration, was told by the Savior, "The ends of the earth shall inquire after thy name, and fools shall have thee in derision, and hell shall rage against thee; while the pure in heart, and the wise, and the noble, and the virtuous, shall seek counsel, and authority, and blessings constantly from under thy hand." (D&C 122:1-2.)

Given Joseph's central role in establishing the Church and the still-prevailing widespread ignorance of Latter-day Saint beliefs and practices, it appears that full accomplishment of at least the second portion of that prophecy lies still in the future. Jesus counseled Joseph, "Be patient in afflictions, for thou shalt have many." (D&C 24:8.) Although persecution and opposition were Joseph's daily lot from the very moment he first spoke of the wondrous vision that ushered in the last dispensation, it is interesting to note that some of the honorable people of the world are beginning to accord to the Prophet the prestige and acclaim that are rightfully his. Some of the misinformation about Joseph is beginning to give way to more enlightened views about his accomplishments. One who appreciates the prophet is Professor Harold Bloom, an immensely learned Jewish intellectual who is Sterling Professor of Humanities at Yale University and Berg Professor of English at New York University. In a strikingly bold and important book entitled *The American Religion: The Emergence of the Post Christian Nation* (New York: Simon and

Schuster, 1992), Professor Bloom has this to say, among other things, about Joseph Smith.

> Smith was an authentic religious genius, unique in our national history. (P. 82.)
>
> I . . . do not find it possible to doubt that Joseph Smith was an authentic prophet. Where in all of American history can we find his match? . . . In proportion to his importance and his complexity, he remains the least-studied personage, of an undiminished vitality, in our entire national saga. (P. 95.)
>
> There is no other figure remotely like him in our entire national history and it is unlikely that anyone like him ever can come again. . . . So rich and varied a personality, so vital a spark of divinity, is almost beyond the limits of the human, as normally we construe those limits. To one who does not believe in him, but who has studied him intensely, Smith becomes almost a mythology in himself. . . . I end as I began, with wonder. We do not know Joseph Smith, as he prophesied that even his own could never . . . know him. He requires strong poets, major novelists, accomplished dramatists to tell his history, and they have not yet come to him. He is as enigmatic as Abraham Lincoln, his contemporary, but even if we do not know Lincoln, we at least keep learning what it is that we cannot quite understand. But with Joseph Smith, we cannot be certain precisely what baffles us most. (Pp. 126–27.)

I marvel at Professor Blooms's deep, though somewhat flawed, insights into Joseph Smith's unique genius, in spite of his inability to discern the source of that genius. Truly, the "foolishness of God is wiser than men; and the weakness of God is stronger than men. . . . God hath chosen the foolish things of the world to confound the wise; and God hath chosen the weak things of the world to confound the things which are mighty . . . that no flesh should glory in his presence." (1 Corinthians 1:25–29.)

In his ode to the Prophet Joseph, Clinton F. Larson attributes these words about Joseph to his mother, Lucy Mack Smith:

He came to me from the fields,
The gold of the grain in his eye,
And soon he was beyond me,
Having seen the white sea of light
Where angels are.

(*The Prophet* [Provo, Utah: Eugene H.
Chapman, 1971], p. 33.)

Though Joseph truly is far beyond us, those who look upon his life and accomplishments with the eyes of faith and love know the source of his power: he was and is a mighty prophet of the living God. We must do more—much more—to proclaim to the world the wondrous truths Joseph and his successors have pronounced. Only when Joseph's message has penetrated every continent and sounded in every ear, as men and women everywhere learn of the Restoration, will the Church be raised up from obscurity. We know that once they hear our message, many will join with us. Many will aid in the redemption of Zion. "For there are many yet on the earth among all sects, parties, and denominations, who are blinded by the subtle craftiness of men, whereby they lie in wait to deceive, and who are only kept from the truth because they know not where to find it." (D&C 123:12.)

That sacred work of gathering people to the truth of God has only just begun. We must redouble our efforts and then double them again.

I return to the other definitions of obscurity, which connote darkness. In that context, to raise the Church up out of darkness is to separate it from the spiritual darkness of the world, as a beam of light penetrates and splits asunder the gloom of night. The Savior's words to Thomas B. Marsh come to mind: "Darkness covereth the earth, and gross darkness the minds of the people, and all flesh has become corrupt before my face. Behold, vengeance cometh speedily upon the inhabitants of the earth." (D&C 112:23-24.)

In no aspect of our national life is that darkness more manifest than in the appalling tragedy besetting American children. In a recent special report entitled *Children in Crisis*, the editors of *Fortune* magazine dealt at length with what is happening to our kids. I quote from an article by Louis S. Richman (*Fortune*, August 10, 1992, pp. 34–36):

> If the well-being of its children is the proper measure of the health of civilization, the United States is in grave danger. Of the 65 million Americans under 18, fully 20% live in poverty, 22% live in single-parent homes, and almost 3% live with no parent at all. Violence among the young is so rampant that the American Academy of Pediatrics calls it a public health emergency.
>
> The loss of childhood innocence is a recent phenomenon, affecting all income levels and all ethnic groups. Playground fights that used to end in bloody noses now end in death. Schools that once considered talking in class a capital offense are routinely frisking kids for weapons, questioning them about drugs. AIDS has turned youthful experimentation with sex into Russian roulette. A good public education, safe streets, and family dinners—with both mother and father present—seem like quaint memories of a far distant past. The bipartisan National Commission on Children wrote in "Beyond Rhetoric," its 1991 report, that addressing the unmet needs of American youngsters "is a national imperative as compelling as an armed attack or a natural disaster."

These facts, presented by Mr. Richman, underline the nature and extent of the problem::

> Every day, more than 25% of women giving birth, 2,900 in all, will have received no prenatal care in the first trimester of their pregnancies. And 25% of that group will have had late care or none at all. Their babies are far more likely to be under normal

weight, to have learning disabilities, and to die in their first year of life than children who have had prenatal care.

Children under 16 make up the largest group of Americans without medical insurance. And 56% of kids without health insurance live in households with incomes above the poverty line. The U.S. infant mortality rate, 9.8 per 1,000 live births, is higher than that of 19 other industrialized nations, including Spain and Singapore. The proportion of U.S. nonwhite 1-year-olds immunized against polio, measles, and other preventable illnesses lags behind that of 55 other nations, including Iraq and Libya.

The parents of nearly 2,750 children separate or divorce each day. More than half of all white kids and three-quarters of African American children under 18 will spend some part of their childhood in a single-parent household.

Every day more than three children die of injuries inflicted by abusive parents. Nearly 90 kids a day are taken from their parents' custody and added to the overburdened foster care system.

Mothers of children under 6, the fastest growing segment of new entrants to the labor force in the 1980's, struggle to find child care solutions for their 11 million children. Some 1.3 million latchkey kids ages 5 to 14 are left to fend for themselves for much of the day.

The typical 14-year old watches three hours of television daily but does just one hour of homework. During the average school day, more than 2,200 kids drop out. These kids are 3 1/2 times more likely to be arrested and six times more likely to become unmarried parents than those who graduate.

Every day over 500 children ages 10 to 14 begin using illegal drugs, and over 1,000 start drinking alcohol. Nearly half of all middle-schoolers abuse drugs or alcohol, or engage in unprotected sex, or live in poverty.

Over 1,400 teenage girls a day—two thirds of them unmarried—become mothers. Only 60% of these teen moms will earn a high school diploma or its equivalent.

Among 15-19-year-olds, homicide by firearms is the third-leading cause of death for whites, and the leading cause of death for blacks.

Forty-one percent of boys and 24% of girls are able to get a gun on a whim, a national survey found.

The Church, with its divine emphasis on the family, can do much to help solve the crisis in family life that is creating such terrible havoc among our children and threatening the loss of a whole generation. We can help part the curtains of darkness that cover much of the world and let the light of the restored gospel shine into homes and hearts. Our message, that God intended families to be forever, that no society can long survive without strong families, and that no other success can compensate for failure in the home, must sound and resound in every ear in America and every other nation.

The Latter-day Saints, above all others, should know and must proclaim to the world that families are ordained by God as the fundamental unit of society and of the Church. Of all social organizations, only the family extends into the eternities. Families were created to enable the members thereof to work together and connect with each other, regardless of family size or composition. Many families nowadays are not "traditional" two-parent families, but *all* families are intended to be precious instruments in the Lord's hands in helping move His children toward celestial goals. Families want to have and use the skills needed to work and connect with each other, but many lack the know-how to do so. We can provide the needed help.

Latter-day Saint families can share their parenting and family-strengthening skills with non-Mormon families in non-threatening, loving ways without appearing to be self-righteous or smug.

The reader may ask, "This is all well and good, but what does all this have to do with building up Zion?" My answer: A great deal. If we are to become a Zion people, we must demonstrate, in our daily family relationships, that we truly are a covenant people, striving to live God's commandments. We must flee from the wickedness engulfing our world, strengthen our families, and become men and women of Christ. (See Helaman 3:29–30.) We must accept a personal responsibility to assist in the fulfillment of the mission of the Church: "To bring to pass the immortality and eternal life of man." (Moses 1:39.) In so doing, we not only grow in personal purity, experiencing the mighty change that sanctifies and exalts the soul, but we also help others, through our example, to leave Babylon and come to Zion. We must become a great light to the nations, a shining beacon that will lead them out of the darkness and obscurity of the world. As the Savior said: "Ye are the light of the world. A city that is set on an hill cannot be hid. Neither do men light a candle, and put it under a bushel, but on a candlestick; and it giveth light unto all that are in the house. Let your light so shine before men, that they may see your good works, and glorify your Father which is in heaven." (Matthew 5:14–16.)

The redemption of Zion, then, requires a people whose goodness shines in their faces and is confirmed by their actions. If we, the Latter-day Saints, who live in general so far below our potential, truly had the light of the gospel in our faces, had we "his image in [our] countenances" (Alma 5:14), the good and righteous from all nations would flock to join us. We have far to go before we reach that ideal.

Where much is given, much is expected (see Luke 12:48), and God will hold us responsible for the choices we make regarding the gifts He has given us, personally and as a people. As President Spencer W. Kimball proclaimed, if we are to become pure in heart, we must "forsake the things of the world as ends in themselves; . . . leave off idolatry and press forward in faith; [and] carry the gospel to our enemies, that they might no longer be our enemies." (*Ensign*, June 1976, pp. 3–6.) God expects even more from us; we must consecrate our time, talents, and all that He gives to us for the building up of Zion. We must work and serve unitedly and with a single heart, striving always to qualify ourselves to dwell in the company of the Father and His glorious Son. Only then can we be pure in heart. And only then can Zion be redeemed.

Chapter Three

Preach Pure Principles

Zion, the pure in heart, can be built up only through the teaching and application of pure principles. Anything less must lead inevitably to results that fall short of the celestial ideal. As the ancient alchemists failed in their misguided attempts to transmute baser elements into gold, so, too, will attempts to build up Zion fail unless the builders teach and practice pure principles. Gold cannot come from lead!

God has given to The Church of Jesus Christ of Latter-day Saints a unique responsibility to bring His truths to the world—to preach the pure principles that underlie and overarch a Zion society. As we long for the day when Zion will be established, we must ever hold dear our sacred responsibility to preach pure principles.

THE STRENGTH OF OUR POSITION

The impression weighs heavily upon me that some of us perhaps do not yet fully understand our own strength as a church and kingdom. In the midst of confusion and commotion, ours is the certain trumpet. In a world of waning conviction, ours is the clarion call of clear testimony. Our message speaks to the deepest longings of the human heart in a way that no other can. To people everywhere who long for the truth but know not where to find it, our words go forth in purity and power: "Come unto Christ . . . and partake of the power of his redemption. Yea, come unto him, and offer your whole souls as an offering unto him, . . . and as the Lord liveth ye will be saved." (Omni 1:26.)

What is the source of the world's confusion and uncertainty, and of our strength? In briefly recounting some aspects of the gulf that separates us from other Christians, I take no pleasure from the discomfiture and loss of direction being experienced by many of our Christian brethren. For all its faults and shortcomings, the Christian church has blessed the lives of countless millions for untold generations, giving them faith and hope for the future. In every age, good and humble people of all classes have worshiped God as best they knew Him, sought spiritual reassurance, and practiced charity toward others. Much of the world's great art, literature, and architecture owes its existence to the Christian church, which kept the lamp of civilization lit for centuries. All Christian churches have some measure of the truth. Our missionaries find their work much easier in Christian countries where the people, though their knowledge of Christ is at best incomplete, at least acknowledge Him as the Son of God.

Sadly, I think, there is a growing sense among many thoughtful observers that we are witnessing the demise or at least the rendering irrelevant of large portions of so-called mainline Christianity. A poignant example underlines my point: A friend who is deeply involved with interfaith activities talked recently with a prominent Protestant clergyman. The clergyman spoke with regret of what he considered to be the deplorable state of affairs in his church. Membership nationally has decreased steadily over the past decade, and the church is riven by internal dissension over doctrine, social policy, and governance. The shortage of funds needed to carry out

various aspects of the church's ministry has reached crisis propor-
tions. A commission has been appointed to study the matter and
make recommendations. "I know," said the clergyman, "that we
could learn much from the Mormon example of paying tithes and
from the way in which the Mormon Church is governed. But rather
than do so there are many among us who would rather see our
church disappear."

What separates us so firmly and fully from our Christian brothers
and sisters and at the same time provides us with such great strength
of position? Simply put, our doctrines, the principles we preach, differ from those of others in ways that cannot be reconciled. Both
views cannot be correct. Time permits discussion of only some of
the many differences between the principles taught by The Church
of Jesus Christ of Latter-day Saints and the philosophies of men,
mingled with scripture, that comprise the creeds of the world.

1. Authority

Much of the Protestant world no longer has a great deal to say
about authority. At the most, vague reference may be made to a universal priesthood of all believers. Roman Catholics believe that
Protestants departed from the true faith, but many who know even a
little about the excesses of the Renaissance popes (among many others) find it hard to accept as valid the claims of the Catholic Church
that it is Christ's church and that the pope is "Christ's Vicar." From
roughly 1470 to 1530, six popes, from Sixtus IV to Clement VII, carried the papacy to "an excess of venality, amorality, avarice, and
spectacularly calamitous power politics. Their governance dismayed
the faithful, brought the Holy See into disrepute, left unanswered the
cry for reform . . . and ended by breaking apart the unity of
Christendom." (Barbara Tuchman, *The March of Folly* [New York:

Ballantine Books, 1984], p. 52; for further detail, see pp. 53–126. See also William Manchester, *A World Lit Only By Fire* [Boston: Little, Brown, and Co., 1992], pp. 74–86.)

The erosion of ecumenicism has taken its toll in the Protestant world. If doctrinal diversity is tolerated between churches, usually by refusing to address the major doctrinal differences that do indeed exist between denominations, then it becomes an embarrassment to dwell on authority. If doctrinal differences are ignored or papered over, if all equally devalue authority and its importance, then to speak of differences is simply to raise awkward questions. We—The Church of Jesus Christ of Latter-day Saints—are bold in our assertions about the need for authority. Our fifth Article of Faith puts the issue clearly: "We believe that a man must be called of God, by prophecy, and by the laying on of hands by those who are in authority, to preach the Gospel and administer in the ordinances thereof." Not only do we assert that valid authority is required, that God insists on more than good intentions in the conduct of *His* work—but we go even further. In claiming that we have the authority to act validly for God, we reject similar claims by all other religious groups. We state unequivocally, quoting Jehovah Himself, that The Church of Jesus Christ of Latter-day Saints is "the only true and living church upon the face of the whole earth, with which [the Lord is] well pleased, speaking unto the church collectively and not individually." (D&C 1:30.)

Furthermore, we believe, and boldly state, that traditional Christianity lost its authority after the death of the New Testament apostles. Christ promised Peter keys and authority, it is true (Matthew 16:19); but, in our view, those keys were apostolic in nature and could be exercised validly and in a binding fashion only by those who bore the holy apostleship. In the years after the death of the apostles, the church suffered a loss of divine authority. It changed as philosophers and theologians mixed the simple principles of the gospel with pagan philosophical systems, such as gnosticism, which taught (among other heresies) that the physical world is evil and therefore that Christ could not have soiled himself by existing in a physical body.

The Apostle Paul is an early witness of the forces that were eroding the foundations of the church within less than two decades after the death and resurrection of Christ. In nearly every letter of Paul, we read of his deep concerns for the future of the church. Examples include the following:

To the Galatians: "I marvel that ye are so soon removed from him that called you into the grace of Christ unto another gospel." (Galatians 1:6.) "But there be some that trouble you, and would pervert the Gospel of Christ." (Galatians 1:7.)

To the Corinthians: "Now I beseech you, brethren, . . . that there be no divisions among you." (1 Corinthians 1:10.) "I hear that there be divisions among you." (1 Corinthians 11:18.) "For such are false apostles, deceitful workers, transforming themselves into the apostles of Christ." (2 Corinthians 11:13.)

To the Ephesians: "Have no fellowship with the unfruitful works of darkness." (Ephesians 5:11.)

To the Philippians: "Beware of dogs, beware of evil workers, beware of the concision." (Philippians 3:2.) (*Concision* means "cutting into pieces, separating.")

To the Colossians: "Beware lest any man spoil you through philosophy and vain deceit, after the tradition of men, . . . and not after Christ." (Colossians 2:8.)

To the Thessalonians: "For the mystery of iniquity doth already work." (2 Thessalonians 2:7; see also verses 2–4.)

To Timothy: "In the latter times some shall depart from the faith, giving heed to seducing spirits, and doctrines of devils." (1 Timothy

4:1–3.) "In the last days perilous times shall come." (2 Timothy 3:1.)
"For the time will come when they will not endure sound doctrine;
. . . and they shall turn away their ears from the truth." (2 Timothy
4:3–4.)

To Titus: "For there are many unruly and vain talkers and
deceivers . . . whose mouths must be stopped, who subvert whole
houses, teaching things which they ought not, for filthy lucre's sake."
(Titus 1:10–11.)

To the Hebrews: "Therefore we ought to give the more earnest
heed to the things which we have heard, lest at any time we should
let them slip." (Hebrews 2:1.)

A generation ago Latter-day Saints spoke and taught and
preached often about "the Great Apostasy." We don't do that as
much nowadays. Perhaps we should say more about this vital matter. Our claim that the Church is a revelatory restoration requires that
there have been an apostasy, a falling away from the truth. There can
be no restoration unless something has been lost. In his first vision,
Joseph Smith was told by Christ that all existing churches lacked the
fullness of the gospel. All had drifted from the truth in their teachings and practices; though they had "a form of godliness," they
denied "the power thereof" and taught "for doctrines the commandments of men." (Joseph Smith–History 1:19.) Thus, for the Church
to have validity in God's sight, it was necessary that a restoration
take place.

Our blunt assertion that the Christian church, bereft of its apostolic leadership, drifted from its moorings and became something
radically different from the church established by Jesus raises
hackles in the Christian world. Many theologians and clergy still persist in ignoring history! Perhaps that is beginning to change. As
Bruce Hafen noted at the 1992 Sperry Symposium at Brigham
Young University, it is interesting that the prestigious *Harvard*

Theological Review recently published an article by a BYU scholar, David Paulsen, that sets forth the belief of the early Christian church that God has a body. Perhaps there is some hope that evidence for a Great Apostasy may yet become academically acceptable! The Protestant reformers of the sixteenth century also implicitly accepted the reality of an apostasy, rejecting the authority of the Roman church, calling it "the true Babylon" and identifying the papacy as a pestilence on Christianity. (See Manchester, *A World Lit Only by Fire,* pp. 124–25, 146, 149.)

Most Christians, of course, know little about the schisms and bitter wrangling that divided the medieval church and led to Catholics killing Protestants and vice versa as well as widespread internecine warfare between rival Protestant groups. Befuddled by the anesthetic haze of ecumenicism and enamored by the siren song of a social gospel that increasingly emphasizes love of neighbor to the exclusion of love and worship of God, they prefer to largely ignore their deep doctrinal differences. Some, perhaps, are unwilling to probe too deeply into the subject, fearing that what they discover may shake their faith.

Blunt talk about the historical reality of the apostasy, the need for a restoration, and the importance of authority if our works and sacraments are to be recognized as valid by God may indeed ruffle some feelings. Yet the facts speak for themselves; they are not of our making. In boldly proclaiming our position, we recognize, of course, that although the Christian church for nearly two millennia did not enjoy divine authority, the Light of Christ, which lighteth every man who is born into the world (see John 1:9, Moroni 7:18–19, D&C 93:2), continued to shine in people's hearts during the long, dark night of the Apostasy. In every generation were men and women of faith who wore out their lives doing good and following Christ insofar as they knew Him. Brigham Young emphasized that before the

Restoration, good people had "the spirit of revelation." (*Journal of Discourses,* 7:5.) He also noted that John Wesley, the great religious reformer and evangelist of the eighteenth century, was as good a man "as ever walked on this earth." (Ibid.)

Though we should always be kind and nonjudgmental in speaking with those not of our faith of the need for authority, we must, I submit, be bold in our assertion that there was a Great Apostasy from the truth, that the fullness of the gospel was restored at the hands of the Prophet Joseph Smith, and that The Church of Jesus Christ of Latter-day Saints, alone among all other religious groups, has the authority to preach the gospel and administer in the ordinances thereof; to bind on earth and have that binding ratified in the heavens.

2. The Nature of God

"It is the first principle of the gospel," said the Prophet Joseph Smith, "to know for a certainty the character of God." (*TPJS,* p. 345.) Knowledge of the nature and character of God was destroyed, we assert, during the long night of the Apostasy. It was restored by two Personages in a pillar of light and these words spoken to the boy Joseph Smith: "This is My Beloved Son. Hear Him!" (Joseph Smith–History 1:17.) More was learned about the character of God in the few minutes of the First Vision than in all the church councils ever called! The creeds of the world were finally canonized only in the fourth and fifth centuries, following long and sterile debates about the nature of the Godhead. The diverse views held today by much of Christendom have gradually evolved from those unenlightened speculations.

Doctrinal confusion about the mission of Christ and His relationship to the Father began within a few years of the Savior's death and resurrection. By the fourth century this confusion had resulted in deep doctrinal schisms within the church. The Emperor Constantine, fearing that the controversy threatened his secular power, particularly in the eastern parts of the Roman Empire, convened the Council of Nicaea in A.D. 325 to try to settle the issue. At its heart, the dispute centered on the nature of Christ. Was He, as some argued, "co-substantial and co-eternal" with the Father? Or was He, as Arius, a prominent churchman from Alexandria in North Africa, claimed, a creation of the Father who "once was not" and was hence intrinsically inferior to His celestial parent? Of the bishops present, many at first sought a vague pronouncement that would commit them to neither side. Eventually, however, the Council condemned Arius and, with reluctance on the part of some participants (who were removed from office and sent into exile by the Emperor Constantine), incorporated the word "homoousios" (one of substance) into the Nicene Creed to signify the equality of the Father and the Son.

A modern English translation of the Greek text of the Nicene Creed contains the following:

> We believe in one God, the Father, the Almighty, maker of heaven and earth, of all that is seen and unseen.
> We believe in one Lord, Jesus Christ, the only Son of God, eternally begotten of the Father, God from God, Light from Light, true God from true God, begotten, not made, one in Being with the Father. Through him all things are made. For us men and for our salvation he came down from heaven: by the power of the Holy Spirit he was born of the Virgin Mary, and became man. . . .
> We believe in the Holy Spirit, the Lord, the giver of life, who proceeds from the Father and the Son. With the Father and the Son he is worshipped and glorified. He has spoken through the prophets. (*Encyclopedia Britannica,* 15th ed., 8:678.)

This creed is accepted as authoritative by Roman Catholic, Eastern Orthodox, Anglican, and major Protestant churches. Without wishing to offend others, I submit that the Creed raises more questions than it answers. It is in reality a mass of confusion that does little to remove the spiritual stumbling blocks that impede true understanding of the nature of the Godhead.

The trinitarian doctrine of the Nicene Creed represents a major departure from the teachings of Jesus and of the early church. Scholars admit that "the . . . doctrine of the Trinity as defined by the great church councils of the fourth and fifth centuries is not to be found in the NT [New Testament]." (*Harper's Bible Dictionary* [New York: Harper and Row, 1985], p. 1099.) Eastern and Western orthodoxies *still* disagree over the precise nature of God. "Beginning in the eighth century and officially since the eleventh century, Roman Catholics [and later Protestants] have added the Latin phrase *Filioque* (and from the Son) to the original text of the 'Nicene Creed' at the point in which that document says that the Holy Spirit proceeds from the Father." (Stephen E. Robinson, *Are Mormons Christian?* [Salt Lake City: Bookcraft, 1991], p. 78.) The Eastern and Western churches split over this issue in the eleventh century—A.D. 1054.

The god of the creeds and councils is the god of the philosophers—abstract; unknowable; incapable of emotion; without body, parts, or passions. Then how could Christ, a God, suffer on the cross as a man would suffer? The Council of Chalcedon (A.D. 451) declared that Christ must have two natures—one human, which suffered on the cross, and the other divine, which felt nothing. Most modern Christians are unaware of this pernicious and evil doctrine. It took two hundred years for the post-Apostolic church to swallow this nonsense about two natures in Christ, and even then the Egyptian,

Abyssinian, Syrian, and Armenian churches couldn't accept it and went their own ways. (Ibid., pp. 82–86.)

Most "ordinary" Christians, unfamiliar with the philosophical theology of the councils, intuitively believe that God is an *actual* father who *really* lives in heaven and *really* loves us. They long for the day, when this life is over, when they can be welcomed into the arms of loved ones and of God Himself. In a survey conducted by Gallup in 1986, 84 percent of Americans asked believed in a personal God who can be reached by prayers. Only 5 percent understood God abstractly as an idea, and 2 percent said He is an impersonal creator. (George Gallup, Jr., and Sarah Jones, *100 Questions & Answers: Religion in America* [Princeton Religion Research Center, 1989], pp. 4–5.) Most Christians do not know the inconsistencies inherent in the official positions of their churches, which offer no serious response to these deeply felt yearnings of heart and soul.

Our knowledge of the character of God stands in stark contrast to the uninspired verbiage of the creeds and councils. God, we assert, is the Father of our spirits. We are His spirit children, created in His image and likeness. We lived with Him before our mortal birth. Elohim, our Father, is an exalted man, a Man of Holiness. (See Moses 6:57.) The Prophet Joseph Smith explained the Father thus: "God himself was once as we are now, and is an exalted man, and sits enthroned in yonder heavens! That is the great secret. If the veil were rent today, the great God who holds this world in its orbit, and who upholds all worlds and all things by his power, was to make himself visible,—I say, if you were to see him today, you would see him like a man in form—like yourselves in all the person, image, and very form as a man." (*TPJS,* p. 345.)

Christ, the only begotten of the Father in the flesh, is our Savior and Redeemer. Through His atoning sacrifice, all things that pertain to life and immortality, to salvation or any rewards hereafter—all these things are given full force and efficacy. The Prophet Joseph, who knew that the Atonement is the central essence of the gospel, said that "all other things [pertaining] to our religion are only appendages to it." (*TPJS,* p. 121.)

We reject the solemn nonsense of the Nicene Creed, with its uninspired notion that the Holy Ghost proceeds forth "from the Father and from the Son." The Holy Ghost, as the scriptures attest and we assert, is a personage of spirit, separate and distinct from the Father and from the Son. He is not one substance with them, though He is perfectly united with them in their work and glory. His special role is to serve as comforter and testator. His companionship is one of the greatest gifts that mortals can enjoy.

And what about those longings of the heart, those impressions of the Spirit felt by so many, that deep desire to be known of and loved by God, to be welcomed into heaven by His loving arms? The God of the creeds and councils, the God of the mainline Christian churches, cannot provide that tender assurance of His love. Their God is inscrutable; unknowable; without body, parts, and passions. Many of their theologians have little faith that heaven exists at all.

For all of our history, Latter-day Saint beliefs on the nature and character of God have been dismissed with contempt by other churches. Mormons, they say, are ignoramuses, know-nothings, whose views on God and our relationship to Him are not worthy of respect and are certainly not Christian. If to be Christian requires acceptance of the God of the creeds and councils, I agree; we don't qualify. But the real question is who is in error, the Latter-day Saints or other Christians? To us there is and can be no question; we reject the unknown and unknowable God of the philosophers but wet with our tears the feet of the loving Father who spoke to the Prophet Joseph.

The misguided views of other churches that Mormon beliefs

about God are not worthy of respect may be changing. A year ago this last summer I was asked by senior representatives of a major Protestant denomination if we—that is, The Church of Jesus Christ of Latter-day Saints—would enter into dialogue with them on the nature of God. It says much about the good and honorable people who made the offer that, by their own admission, they have been so preoccupied with internal troubles that they have not been able to follow up on their proposal.

Significantly, it is the latter-day scriptures that tell us most clearly of God's loving arms outstretched to welcome us home. Two examples will make the point: From D&C 6:20: "Be faithful . . . and I will encircle thee in the arms of my love." And Lehi's words from 2 Nephi 1:15: "The Lord hath redeemed my soul . . . ; I am encircled about eternally in the arms of his love."

Being clasped in the arms of the Savior symbolizes the fulfillment of His atonement in our lives. Through the Atonement we belong to Him: "Inasmuch as ye have received me, ye are in me and I in you." (D&C 50:43.)

3. Ordinances and Covenants

The saving and exalting ordinances of the gospel are inextricably intertwined with the sacred covenants. No covenant is given unless it is associated with an ordinance, and vice versa. If a covenant is a sacred promise, an ordinance is a sacred act, carried out (if it is to be effective) by one who has divine authority to do so. In the absence of the proper authority, the actions involved in performing an ordinance become at best a solemn charade, form without substance, pageantry without purpose. Unless divinely sanctioned, changes in the sacred ordinances result in men and women being led into dreadful error that imperils their immortal souls. So important are the ordinances that the devil works hard to have people change them, trivialize them, and make them seem less important. He knows that if he can make people think of the ordinances as largely meaningless ritual, he will weaken commitment to the sacred covenants associated with them. Alternatively, he may elect to have the ordinances associated with such pomp and pageantry that they take on a life of their own; then people do not look beyond them to the covenants they symbolize.

The importance of the ordinances is underlined by Isaiah's solemn reminder of cause and effect in human affairs. In describing the latter-days, he said, "The earth also is defiled under the inhabitants thereof; because they have transgressed the laws, changed the ordinance, broken the everlasting covenant." (Isaiah 24:5.) In a "voice of warning . . . unto all people," Jehovah Himself declared, "The anger of the Lord is kindled, and his sword is bathed in heaven, and it shall fall upon the inhabitants of the earth. And the arm of the Lord shall be revealed; and the day cometh that they who will not hear the voice of the Lord, neither the voice of his servants, neither give heed to the words of the prophets and apostles, shall be cut off from among the people; for they have strayed from mine ordinances, and have broken mine everlasting covenant; they seek not the Lord to establish his righteousness, but every man walketh in his own way, and after the image of his own god." (D&C 1:13–16.) Woe be unto those who tamper with the sacred ordinances, for great shall be their fall! Yet tampering is just what has happened.

Baptism, A Case Study in Tampering

The baptism of Jesus by John the Baptist (see Mark 1:9–11) set the divinely approved pattern for the future administration of this sacred ordinance. In the early Church, candidates were baptized on their acceptance of the gospel message. (See Acts 8:35–39.) By the beginning of the third century, however, formal instruction, sometimes lasting up to three years, was required. The period for preparing candidates for baptism before Easter became formalized into the forty days of Lent. By that time baptism, though still by immersion, required the candidate to confess faith in each member of the Trinity, with immersion after each confession. Gregory the Great, Bishop of Rome from 590–604, approved a single immersion, but some Eastern churches have preserved the practice of immersing the candidate for baptism three times.

The precedent of Jewish washings (see Leviticus 14–15), circumstantial accounts of baptism in the early Christian literature, and the symbolism of baptism as burial and resurrection (Romans 6:1–11) suggest strongly that, in the early church, baptism involved complete immersion, or dipping of the entire person. However, by the second century, the *Didache*, a manual of church life included among the works of the Apostolic Fathers, permitted pouring water three times on the head instead of complete immersion.

The earliest extant reference to infant baptism is from about the year 200; infant baptism seems at that time to have been a relatively new practice. By the fifth century, infant baptism was common; it received great impetus from the doctrine of original sin propounded by Augustine and was made compulsory by the Emperor Justinian in the sixth century. Early Christian documents, in contrast, contain frequent references to the sinlessness of children. Furthermore, the word of the Lord on the matter, given to the Prophet Mormon, is as follows: "I came into the world not to call the righteous but sinners to repentance; the whole need no physician, but they that are sick; wherefore, little children are whole, for they are not capable of committing sin; wherefore the curse of Adam is taken from them in me, that it hath no power over them; and the law of circumcision is done away in me." (Moroni 8:8.)

Speaking further on the baptism of children, Mormon explained:

After this manner did the Holy Ghost manifest the word of God unto me; wherefore, my beloved son, I know that it is solemn mockery before God, that ye should baptize little children.

Behold I say unto you that this thing shall ye teach—repentance and baptism unto those who are accountable and capable of committing sin; yea, teach parents that they must repent and be baptized, and humble themselves as their little children, and they shall all be saved with their little children.

And their little children need no repentance, neither baptism. Behold, baptism is unto repentance to the fulfilling the commandments unto the remission of sins. But little children are alive in Christ, even from the foundation of the world; if not so, God is a partial God, and also a changeable God, and a respecter to persons; for how many little children have died without baptism!

Wherefore, if little children could not be saved without baptism, these must have gone to an endless hell.

Behold I say unto you, that he that supposeth that little children need baptism is in the gall of bitterness and in the bonds of iniquity; for he hath neither faith, hope, nor charity; wherefore, should he be cut off while in the thought, he must go down to hell.

For awful is the wickedness to suppose that God saveth one child because of baptism, and the other must perish because he hath no baptism.

Woe be unto them that shall pervert the ways of the Lord after this manner, for they shall perish except they repent. Behold, I speak with boldness, having authority from God; and I fear not what man can do; for perfect love casteth out all fear." (Moroni 8:9–16.)

Information on baptism in the early Christian church is found in *The Eerdmans Bible Dictionary*, Allen C. Myers, ed. (Grand Rapids, Michigan: William B. Eerdmans Publishing Co., 1987), pp. 123–24, and extensively in *Encyclopedia of Early Christianity*, Everett Ferguson, ed. (New York: Garland Publishing, 1990), pp. 131–34.

Ordinances of the Temple

The ordinances of the temple are unique to the Latter-day Saints. Other religious groups have nothing like them; they simply do not understand why we build and use temples. Yet the Prophet Joseph Smith explained, "The main object [of gathering the people of God in any age of the world] was to build unto the Lord a house whereby he could reveal unto his people the ordinances of his house and the glories of his kingdom, and teach the people the way of salvation; for there are certain ordinances and principles that, when they are taught and practiced, must be done in a place or house built for that purpose." (*TPJS* p. 308.)

Only in the temple do we receive and are we blessed by the fullness of the holy priesthood. "If a man gets a fullness of the priesthood of God," the Prophet explained, "he has to get it in the same way that Jesus Christ obtained it, and that was by keeping all the commandments and obeying all the ordinances of the house of the Lord." (*Ibid.*)

In the temple we receive the sacred, redeeming ordinances essential for the building up of a Zion people. There we enter into covenants to consecrate our lives to the furthering of the Lord's work upon the earth and to the development and righteous use of talents that He has given us. The Lord Himself has explained that the purpose of building temples is to reveal the ordinances: "Let this house be built unto my name, that I may reveal mine ordinances therein unto my people." (D&C 124:40.) Through the sacred ordinances "the power of godliness is manifest." (D&C 84:20.) In the temple the sealing power of the priesthood is exercised. Celestial marriage—the sealing together of man and woman for time and all eternity—with its promise not only of continuance but of eternal increase, is the crowning gospel ordinance, administered only in the holy temple.

4. Revelation

Our Christian friends in other denominations believe that the canon of scripture is closed, the heavens are sealed, and revelation has ceased. The "Westminster Confession of Faith" (6.006, *Book of Confessions*, Presbyterian Church, USA) states, "The whole counsel of God, concerning all things necessary for his own glory, man's salvation, faith, life, is either expressly set down in scripture, or by good and necessary consequence, may be deduced from scripture: unto which nothing at any time is to be added, whether by new revelation of the spirit, or traditions of men." Nearly every other Protestant denomination has a similar confession of faith, and the Roman Catholic encyclicals on the matter use similar language. I doubt that most "ordinary" Christians even know that their church teaches that God no longer speaks to his children.

It hardly needs mentioning that if the heavens are closed, if God speaks no more, there is no need for a prophet to serve as God's mouthpiece to the world. No revelation, no prophet; the conclusion is inevitable.

Is God then dead, as prominent Protestant theologians have suggested, or does He no longer care for us? It was of such a false God that the Prophet Elijah spoke when he mocked the priests of Baal: "Either [Baal] is talking, or he is pursuing, or he is in a journey, or peradventure he sleepeth, and must be awaked." (1 Kings 18:27.) An absentee God will never meet the needs of His children.

In contrast to the sterile confessions of faith accepted by other Christian churches, we proclaim boldly that God lives, that His love for His children has not grown cold, that He continues to reveal His will through His holy prophets. We are one with Amos, the Old Testament prophet: "Surely the Lord God will do nothing, but he revealeth his secret unto his servants the prophets." (Amos 3:7.) We profess to believe "all that God has revealed, all that He does now reveal, and we believe that He will yet reveal many great and important things pertaining to the Kingdom of God." (Article of Faith 9.)

To us it is not logical that God would speak to a series of prophets, from Adam onwards and then, suddenly, capriciously, simply cease further communications forever. His message to Abraham did not suffice for Moses. Nor did His whisperings to Moses suffice for Isaiah, or Jeremiah, or all others who lived after Moses. Each prophet brings to the world the instructions and encouragement needed for his time. Our world of the late twentieth century, with problems never dreamed of by the ancients, needs modern revelation, delivered through living prophets.

The need for modern revelation is succinctly summarized in these words of President Joseph F. Smith:

> Are we to understand, then, that God does not, and will not further make known his will to men; that what he has said suffices? His will to Moses and Isaiah and John is abundant for modern followers of Christ? The Latter day Saints take issue with this doctrine, and pronounce it illogical, inconsistent, and untrue, and bear testimony to all the world that God lives and that he reveals his will to men who believe in him and who obey his commandments, as much in our day as at any time in the history of nations. The canon of scripture is not full. God has never revealed at any time that he would cease to speak forever to men. If we are permitted to believe that he has spoken, we must and do believe that he continues to speak, because he is unchangeable. (*Gospel Doctrine*, pp. 36–37.)

In their canons of scripture, our Christian friends do not, of course, include the Book of Mormon or the other Restoration scriptures. They speak only of the Bible, conveniently omitting to mention that disputes still remain as to which books should be included in that holy work. Historically, there has not been one Christian canon but many. A copy of the list of books then accepted as canonical by the church in Rome, written about A.D. 200, was discovered by Lodovico Muratori in the year 1740 in the Ambrosian Library in Milan. The list is called The Muratorian Canon. It indicates that the Roman church of the late second century did not consider the books of Hebrews, James, 1 Peter, or 2 Peter to be scripture. Two of the letters of John were accepted, although scholars are not sure which; and two works now not included in the New Testament, the Apocalypse of Peter and the Wisdom of Solomon, were then considered scripture, by people who everyone would agree were Christians. (*Encyclopedia of Early Christianity*, Everett Ferguson, ed. [New York: Garland Publishing, 1990], p. 628.)

Despite what other Christians may think, the prophets have reminded us often that the Book of Mormon will bring men and women to God with a power unequaled by any other portion of Holy Writ. It holds a special place in the hearts of Latter-day Saints as the "keystone of our religion" and as "Another Testament of Jesus Christ."

We also teach and preach that the Holy Bible is the word of God insofar as it has been correctly translated. Why the concern about biblical translations?

Wise Nephi, who understood so well the importance of pure principles, foresaw that numerous "plain and precious things" would be taken from the Bible, causing many who read it to stumble in spiritual gloom. (See 1 Nephi 13.) Some truths were lost through malignant tampering, others through uninspired textual alterations during transcribing or translation. Although the process clearly was incremental in nature, it appears that most of the doctrinal damage occurred during the hundred years from about the second half of the first century to the middle of the second century as the church, increasingly bereft of apostolic leadership and authority, compromised its beliefs to become more attractive to the world. (See Stephen E. Robinson, "Warring Against the Saints of God," *Ensign*, January 1988, pp. 38–39.)

The adversary, who knows the scriptures well, puts his major emphasis on corrupting and perverting the principles that are of greatest importance to the spiritual well-being of mankind. He knows that he will win if he can excise the foundation principles from the scriptures or so pervert and corrupt them that they lose spiritual power and validity. *The more important the principle, the more assiduous his efforts to remove it.* Failing that, he will try to discredit the principle, to make of it an object of derision, or to substitute his own clever counterfeit version and thus lead the children of God astray.

So universal is this attempt by Satan to corrode and pervert the fundamental truths that one test of what constitutes a fundamental principle may well be the evidence that significant change has occurred in the understanding of it over time. In some instances so many "plain and precious" truths have been lost that the world's understanding of the principle is either nonexistent or seriously corrupted. It follows, too, that greater fullness of exposition and clarity of explanation of each of the foundation principles will be found in the Restoration scriptures and words of the living prophets than in the Holy Bible.

A WORD OF CAUTION

God has given us the awesome responsibility to bring the fullness of His revealed gospel to all the world. I hope as we do so we will ever remember that the message we bring resolves Christianity's "doctrinal dilemmas" and restores to the world precious truths lost or taken away during darker days. Our message, as Bruce Hafen said recently, is "the last and best and only hope of Christianity and of all mankind." (*Church News*, October 3, 1992, p. 7.) It answers the deepest yearnings of the human heart. It provides the answers for which millions of the elect seek but which cannot be found elsewhere.

At the same time, as we go forth in boldness, secure in the knowledge that we are the Lord's agents, on His errand, let us pray daily for humility. *We have no monopoly on goodness.* Perhaps of all people, we live far below our privileges. There are so many good people not of our faith—both clergy and laity—who put us to shame by their Christian charity, their desire to follow Christ, and their noble examples.

Nor should we be judgmental about the Great Apostasy and the falling away that occurred. Let us view it with sadness, reminding ourselves that we, too, are fallible, foolish mortals, that none is immune from the wiles of the devil. Above all, let us consider all men and women everywhere as our brothers and sisters. May we remind ourselves often that God "hath made of one blood all nations of men for to dwell on all the face of the earth." (Acts 17:26.) There is much more that should bring us together as sons and daughters of God than ought to drive us apart. Let us, then, do good to all and see and pay tribute to the good in all, remembering always who we are and what God expects of us as keepers of a sacred trust.

In the spirit of charity—the pure love of Christ—let us practice and preach respect and tolerance for others. The Prophet Joseph Smith gave a great lesson for all in the theory and practice of respect when he said the following at Nauvoo in 1843:

The Saints can testify whether I am willing to lay down my life for my brethren. If it has been demonstrated that I have been willing to die for a "Mormon," I am bold to declare before Heaven that I am just as ready to die in defending the rights of a Presbyterian, a Baptist, or a good man of any other denomination; for the same principle which would trample upon the rights of the Latter-day Saints would trample upon the rights of the Roman Catholics, or of any other denomination who may be unpopular and too weak to defend themselves. (*History of the Church*, 5:498.)

But, some may say, if we are to be charitable toward others, surely we must avoid criticizing their actions. To the contrary, if we truly love others we are under solemn obligation to warn them, lovingly and with sensitivity, of the danger they are in if they persist in ways that depart grievously from the truth. An article in *Times and Seasons* puts it this way:

Charity in the full sense of the word is the love of God shed abroad in the hearts of the people of God; love towards your neighbors; assistance and friendship in the time of distress and danger. For instance we see a person in danger, and he ignorant of it, it would not be charity in us to flatter him in his dangerous condition, and thus expose him to more danger, or in other words, if any person is deceived, and is in a dangerous condition, and we know his condition to be an awful one; it is charity in us, not only that, but it is our duty to warn him of his danger and entreat him to forsake the evil way, instead of acknowledging his delusion to be good, and thus flatter him in wickedness. (*Times and Seasons*, December 15, 1841, p. 628.)

The author continues:

Now if Christ and the apostles had the same kind of charity that the people want us to have, they would have said to the Pharisees, Sadducees, Scribes, Alexandrians, Syrenians, etc., go on, you are doing well; this difference of opinion is only of minor consequence. And if they had thus flattered them, what would have been the consequence? Would it not have involved them deeper in sin and iniquity, and caused them to drink a greater draft of the intoxicating spirit of delusion, and encouraged them in their works of darkness? Let the reader answer this question for himself. It certainly was pure charity that inspired Christ and his apostles to reprove the world for their sins, and corruptions; and why should it be considered an uncharitable act in the Latter-day Saints to do the same, providing the world are in similar circumstances? (Ibid., p. 629.)

Let us then go forward boldly to proclaim our message—in power, purity, and personal humility—to the world. Our doctrines, the principles we espouse, differ substantially from those of other Christian churches. We do neither ourselves nor others a favor by papering over those differences, pretending they don't exist or are of no account. At the same time, however, let us be governed in our words and actions by pure charity, showing unfeigned tolerance and respect toward all of God's children. A mark of the Zion people of God is their willingness and eagerness to love those who oppose them.

Chapter Four

Stewards over Earthly Blessings

In a revelation concerning the United Order given to the Prophet Joseph Smith in April 1834, the Lord reminded His Church that every man (and assuredly every woman also) is accountable as a "steward over earthly blessings" that He has made and prepared for His creatures. (D&C 104:13.) The importance and priority of that sacred stewardship are indicated by the fact that our accountability will be given to Christ Himself: "That every man may give an account unto me of the stewardship which is appointed unto him." (D&C 104:12.) When He interviews us, I feel certain that one of His questions will, in essence, be the following: "What have you done with the earth which my Father and I gave you as a home? Have you cherished and protected it? Have you dressed it and kept it, as your father Adam was commanded to do? Or have you laid waste to it, defiled its waters, destroyed its fertile lands, befouled its life-giving air?" To those questions, I fear there are many, even among those who aspire to become a Zion people, who will hang their heads in shame. The earth groans under the insults inflicted upon it.

This is not the place to recount in detail the extent of the environmental damage that in every country poses a major challenge to the future of the world as we know it. Most readers are familiar with at least the daily newspaper headlines, which disturb and perhaps even frighten us but to which we become first accustomed and then calloused. Many others, reacting to the uncertainties inherent in science and the exaggerated claims on one side of environmental issues or another, grow cynical and believe nothing that is written or said on the matter. There is, however, a broad consensus among scientists: details aside, our current way of life is simply environmentally unsustainable. The immensely complex and still not fully understood systems that sustain life on earth are being destroyed by human activities. Consider the following:

• Desertification, the impoverishment and degradation of the land through over-grazing, over-cultivation, deforestation, and faulty irrigation practices, claims an estimated 15 million acres worldwide each year. This represents an area the size of West Virginia lost beyond practical hope of reclamation from its desert-like state, at least in the short-term. An additional 50 million acres annually become too degraded and impoverished to support profitable farming or grazing. West African farmers lament *Kasar mu, ta gaji*, in the Hausa language, "The land is tired." In the African country of Mauritania, there were reportedly 43 sandstorms during the 1960s, but "in 1983 alone a record 240 sandstorms darkened the nation's skies." (*World Watch Reader on Global Environmental Issues* [New York: W. W. Norton and Co., 1991], p. 28.) According to the United Nations, "11 billion acres—35% of the earth's land surface—are threatened by desertification," and with them fully 20 percent of humanity. (Ibid., p. 27.) Man is both the victim and the agent of this unbalanced relationship between people and the land.

• The United States National Research Council estimates that 21 million barrels of oil enter the oceans annually from "street runoff,

ships flushing their tanks, and effluent from industrial facilities."
(Ibid., p. 46.) More than 600,000 barrels are accidentally spilled each
year, on average. In January 1993, the tanker *Braer*, carrying nearly
25 million gallons of Norwegian oil to Canada, went aground on one
of the Shetland Islands, north of Scotland, spilling her cargo into the
sea. As little as "one part of oil for every ten million parts of water
has serious effects on the reproduction and growth of fish, crus-
taceans, and plankton." (Ibid., p. 47.) Every day, merchant ships
dump up to an estimated half million plastic containers into the
seas. In the northern Pacific until very recently, "more than 700
Japanese, South Korean, and Taiwanese fishing boats equipped with
20-to-40-mile-long drift nets [swept] an area the size of Ohio each
night," catching fish, mammals, and birds relatively indiscriminately.
(Ibid., p. 53.)

• As a result of the use of industrial chemicals known as chloro-
fluorocarbons, depletion of the ozone shield, which protects the earth
from harmful solar ultraviolet radiation, is occurring far more rapidly
and is more widespread than anticipated. Already existing degradation of the ozone layer will permit 8 to 12 percent more radiation to
reach the earth, with possible serious effects not only on human
health but also on the planet's food chains, both on land and in the
oceans. The same chemicals that deplete the ozone layer also prevent infrared radiation from escaping it and thus participate in the
global warming (the "greenhouse" effect) that many scientists
believe has already started. "Six of the seven warmest years since
1850 have . . . occurred since 1980." (Ibid., p. 80.) Some scientists
believe that by the year 2030, global average temperatures will be
between two and eight Fahrenheit degrees higher than they averaged
between 1950 and 1980, with possible catastrophic effects on coastal
cities, crop production, and perhaps human life itself.

• United Nations statistics show that more than one billion

people live in areas where air quality has been seriously compromised. In Mexico City, for example, buildings and other landmarks are routinely almost obscured from view by an oily brown haze of pollution arising from millions of people, millions of automobiles, and thousands of industrial activities. Government standards for maximum permitted ozone levels are exceeded in Mexico City more than 300 days per year. And in the United States, factories reported 1.3 million tons of hazardous emissions in 1987.

• "One third of the world's original tropical rain forests are gone, and with them . . . tens of thousands of species" of flora and fauna. (Ibid., p. 170.) The rest are going fast. In 1987 alone, some "20 million acres of virgin Brazilian forest, an area the size of Maine, went up in smoke," according to the Food and Agriculture Organization of the United Nations and the Brazilian National Space Research Institute. (Ibid., p. 171.)

• Widespread contamination of soil and water exists in the former East Germany, resulting from industrial practices associated with cold war activities. Near Oberrothenbach, for example, is a lake that served as a dump for a nearby uranium processing factory. The lake water kills unfortunate animals drinking there, and no wonder: it "contains an estimated 22,500 tons of arsenic—enough to kill everyone in Europe—plus huge amounts of lead, iron, cadmium, sulfuric acid, low-level radioactive materials, and other poisons. And the lake is just a small part of the environmental assault" imposed on that portion of Germany. Some "500 million tons of chemical and low-level radioactive waste are spread over 1200 square kilometers." (*Science*, January 22, 1993, p. 448.)

The above information, taken largely from the respected *World Watch Reader on Global Environmental Issues*, indicates clearly that the concept of trusteeship over the earth has not received sufficient attention from many. A combination of avarice and ignorance has put our earthly home in danger. President Spencer W. Kimball's somber words come to mind: "I have traveled much in various assignments over the years, and when I pass through the lovely countryside or fly over the vast and beautiful expanses of our globe, I compare these beauties with many of the dark, miserable practices of man, and I have the feeling that the good earth can hardly bear our presence upon it. I recall the occasion when Enoch heard the earth mourn, saying, 'Wo, wo is me, the mother of men; I am pained, I am weary, because of the wickedness of my children. When shall I rest, and be cleansed from the filthiness which is gone forth out of me?'" (*Ensign*, June 1976, p. 4; see Moses 7:48.)

THE PROPHETS SPEAK

The views of the prophets are clear on the responsibilities shared by all humankind to protect and watch over the earth, to dress and keep it. Brigham Young, who had a strong commitment to preservation of the environment and the wise use of natural resources, counseled the Saints thus: "There is a great work for the Saints to do. Progress, and improve upon, and make beautiful everything around you. Cultivate the earth and cultivate your minds. Build cities, adorn your habitations, make gardens, orchards, and vineyards, and render the earth so pleasant that when you look upon your labours you may do so with pleasure, and that angels may delight to come and visit your beautiful locations." (*Journal of Discourses,* 8:83.)

The concept of stewardship, of being a trustee over earthly blessings, was never far from President Young's mind. "The blessings of the Lord are great upon this people. . . . The earthly means which we have been enabled to gather around us is not ours, it is the Lord's, and he has placed it in our hands for the building up of his kingdom and to extend our ability and resources for reaching after the poor in other lands." (Ibid., 10:222.) Truly, "the earth is the Lord's, and the fulness thereof" (Psalm 24:1); we are but tenants with a steward's responsibility to look after the earthly blessings with which the Lord has entrusted us, and to pass them on undamaged to our children and grandchildren.

In a thoughtful and sensitive address given at general conference in 1978, President Kimball deplored the unnecessary shedding of blood and destruction of animal life so common in our society, describing the capricious killing of birds and animals as "not only wicked" but also "a shame." (*Ensign*, November 1978, p. 45.) He quoted the Prophet Joseph Smith on this matter as follows:

> We crossed the Embarras river and encamped on a small branch of the same about one mile west. In pitching my tent we found three massasaugas or prairie rattlesnakes, which the brethren were about to kill, but I said, "Let them alone—don't hurt them! How will the serpent ever lose his venom, while the servants of God possess the same disposition and continue to make war upon it? Men must become harmless, before the brute creation; and when men lose their vicious dispositions and cease to destroy the animal race, the lion and the lamb can dwell together, and the sucking child can play with the serpent in safety." The brethren took the serpents carefully on sticks and carried them across the creek. I exhorted the brethren not to kill a serpent, bird, or an animal of any kind during our journey unless it became necessary in order to preserve ourselves from hunger. (*History of the Church,* 2:71–72.)

Note how Joseph differentiates between the justifiable killing of animals for necessary food and their wanton slaughter for pleasure.

How commendable, how wise and far-seeing is the admonition of the prophets that we care for *all* life, holding it in sacred reverence and dealing with it wisely and with affectionate respect. The importance of doing so was noted several years ago by President

Ezra Taft Benson, who concluded that at their core, environmental problems are caused by spiritual deficiencies. As you may recall, President Benson is no stranger to environmental issues, having served with great distinction as Secretary of Agriculture in the United States Government during the Eisenhower administration. He said, "One dimension of spiritual law . . . is that one's self-regard and his esteem for his fellow men are intertwined. If there is a disregard for one's self, there is bound to be some disregard for one's neighbor. If there isn't a reverence for life itself, there is apt to be little reverence for the resources God has placed here on which we must call. The outward expressions of irreverence for God, for life, and for our fellowmen take the form of things like littering, heedless strip-mining, heedless pollution of water and air. But these are, after all, outward expressions of the inner man." ("Problems Affecting the Domestic Tranquility of Citizens of the United States," *Vital Speeches*, February 1, 1976, 42:240.)

There are, I believe, two additional (and interrelated) deficiencies in "the inner man," or perhaps more accurately in the natural man, that contribute mightily to the environmental problems that besmirch and befoul this beautiful earthly home the Lord has given us and, at the same time, impede the development of Zion. They are selfishness and idolatry.

Selfishness, with its associates greed and avarice, puts individual gain over the common good. That attitude places short-term profit over long-term damage to the environment. It takes no thought of tomorrow; it has no concern for those who will inherit the wreckage of today. Those who subscribe to this "slash and burn" attitude will destroy in a year what it took nature a thousand years to build up. Many examples come to mind:

• Commercial logging operations in West Africa that just a few years ago involved the destruction of several acres of rain forest to obtain a handful of large mahogany or other trees that could be sold for large sums of money.

• Strip-mining operations that leave the earth scarred and useless.

• Cities that pour millions of gallons of raw sewage into lakes, streams, and marine bodies of water.

Laws preventing such callous, wanton disregard for the earth are in place in most developed Western countries. Sadly, it is in the poor, developing countries of the world, where there are neither the laws nor the means to enforce them, that the worst destruction now goes on. "They seek not the Lord to establish his righteousness, but every man walketh in his own way, and after the image of his own God, whose image is in the likeness of the world." (D&C 1:16.) "If we insist on spending all our time and resources building up for ourselves a worldly kingdom," President Kimball reminded us, "that is exactly what we will inherit." (*Ensign*, June 1976, p. 6.) Indeed, the devil offers that deal—worldly success in exchange for eternal life— to all who will listen to his lies and deceit. He offered it even to Jesus. (See Matthew 4:3–10.) Those who make such a pact with Satan always lose, of course. "The devil will not support his children at the last day, but doth speedily drag them down to hell." (Alma 30:60.)

Closely allied with selfishness, and often co-existent with it, is the sin of idolatry. Those who worship their possessions, the "gods of silver, and gold, of brass, iron, wood, and stone, which see not, nor hear, nor know" (Daniel 5:23), are unlikely to have much reverence for the earth or the creatures and creations thereon. Trusting in "the arm of flesh," impatient to grasp and gain, they pay little heed to the long-term consequences of their actions.

I well recall being asked several years ago by the then Minister of National Health in Canada to travel to Newfoundland to investigate the cause of massive fish kills in a place called Long Harbor. Fish by the thousands were flinging themselves onto the beaches, writhing and dying in what seemed to be agony, their bodies covered with pin-point ("petechial") hemorrhages. Further investigations showed that the waters of the harbor sheltered essentially no animal life at all. Dead fish were stacked up, like corn in a crib, for depths of thirty to forty feet out in the harbor, and even the lobsters that normally crawled over the seabed were dead, every one of them.

The cause of all this senseless slaughter was not hard to find. A huge facility manufacturing elemental phosphorus from phosphate rock had recently been set up on Long Harbor. After several months of "running-in," the plant was now fully operational. Hundreds of tons of phosphorus were pumped each week out to waiting tankers, to be shipped to England and elsewhere for use in preparing various commodities, notably detergents.

"Tailings" from the manufacturing operation were simply dumped out of a pipe into the sea, fifty feet or so from the end of the dock, which extended five hundred feet or more into the water of the harbor. A great yellow "boil" of elemental phosphorus, twenty feet across, continually bubbled up to the surface of the water. The fish and other creatures dying by the tens of thousands suffered from the classical symptoms of phosphorous poisoning.

When I brought this sorry state of affairs to the attention of the chief engineer at the phosphorous plant, he shrugged his shoulders. "Interesting," he said, "but I couldn't care less; my job is to get this plant 'on line' and to produce 75,000 tons of phosphorus a year. Why should I care about some fish?" His god was technology and the profits it promised; his life, whether he knew it or not, was one of idolatry. (Incidentally, the Canadian government promptly shut down the phosphorous plant until the operators figured out how to run it properly, without endangering all life in the harbor.)

Frankly, I faulted the engineers less than those at the top of the operation who were driven by only one motive: profit. They really didn't care what effect their operations had on the environment so long as the golden idol was fed.

DOMINION OVER THE EARTH

There are some who try to use scriptural arguments to justify disregard for and violation of the earth. "After all," they say, "God gave man 'dominion . . . over all the earth' and commanded Adam and Eve (and hence their descendants) to 'replenish the earth, and subdue it.' [See Genesis 1:26, 28.] Surely those bequeathals provide the necessary authority to do whatever we wish. After all, God gave the world to us, to do with as we please!" How shallow an argument!

Humankind has a clear and certain obligation, in implementing the awesome powers with which God has entrusted us, to act responsibly, as trusted stewards, attempting insofar as is possible to act as our Father would do were He here personally. We are *His* agents, assigned and required to act in *His* name. Our attitudes toward the earth should mirror those of the psalmist:

> "O Lord my God, thou art very great; . . . Who coverest thyself with light as with a garment: who stretchest out the heavens like a curtain: Who layeth the beams of his chambers in the waters: who maketh the clouds his chariot: who walketh upon the wings of the wind: . . .
>
> Who laid the foundations of the earth, that it should not be removed for ever. Thou coveredst it with the deep as with a garment: the waters stood above the mountains. At thy rebuke they fled; at the voice of thy thunder they hasted away. . . .
>
> Thou hast set a bound that they may not pass over; that they turn not again to cover the earth. He sendeth the springs into the valleys, which run among the hills. They give drink to every beast of the field: . . . By them shall the fowls of the heaven have their

habitation. . . . He watereth the hills from his chambers: the earth is satisfied with the fruit of thy works. He causeth the grass to grow for the cattle, and herb for the service of man: that he may bring forth food out of the earth; . . .

O Lord, how manifold are thy works! in wisdom hast thou made them all: the earth is full of thy riches. So is this great and wide sea, wherein are things creeping innumerable, both small and great beasts. . . . There is that leviathan, whom thou hast made to play therein. These wait all upon thee; . . .

Thou hidest thy face, they are troubled: thou takest away their breath, they die, and return to their dust. Thou sendest forth thy spirit, they are created: and thou renewest the face of the earth. The glory of the Lord shall endure for ever: the Lord shall rejoice in his works. (Psalm 104:1–3, 6–14, 24–27, 29–31.)

God's love for and reverence for all life, which must be the pattern for our behavior, is clearly indicated by His personal statement:

And God said, Let the waters bring forth abundantly the moving creature that hath life, and fowl that may fly above the earth in the open firmament of heaven. . . .

And God said, Behold, I have given you every herb bearing seed, which is upon the face of all the earth, and every tree, in the which is the fruit of a tree yielding seed; to you it shall be for meat.

And to every beast of the earth, and to every fowl of the air, and to every thing that creepeth upon the earth, wherein there is life, I have given every green herb for meat: and it was so.

And God saw every thing that he had made, and, behold, it was very good. (Genesis 1:20, 29–31; italics added.)

The dominion over the earth that God gave to humanity is part of the testing program that is a major purpose of our earthly existence. Our Father wishes to determine if we are able to use God-like powers righteously. It is a necessary test, given our divine potential. If we fail it, how can the Father trust us with creations of our own?

In a word, then, humanity's dominion is a call to stewardship, not a license to pillage.

A variation of the "I-can-do-as-I-please" school of thought is the notion that it doesn't matter how badly we treat the earth because Jesus will return soon anyway and make everything right. That, too, is a spurious and specious argument. First of all, the scriptures make it clear that no one knows the time of the Second Coming. Why should we live in a sewer while awaiting Christ's return? Second, does a child have the right to burn down the family home just because his parents possess the ability to rebuild it?

What, then, in practical terms, are we to make of mankind's "dominion over all the earth?" Is it best expressed by leaving the earth as pristine wilderness, untouched by the hand of man? Although there will inevitably be less and less wilderness as the world's population increases, we would do well to preserve as much of it as we can for two important reasons. First, the wilderness is the great producer of the plant and animal species needed to maintain essential biological diversity on the earth. It serves also as the great natural reservoir of renewable resources of materials, pharmaceuticals, energy, and so on.

Second, I believe that humankind, for the sake of its own sanity, needs to maintain a sense of continuity with the past, with its own roots, and with all the rest of God's creations. To do so requires periodic contact with the primeval. Thus, I for one would not wish to live in a world without wilderness. That is not to say, however, that the earth-as-wilderness model comes even close to meeting the entire needs of the human race. The world's peoples need to be fed, clothed, housed, and provided with essential materials and other things that come from the earth. Granted the need to maintain appropriate wilderness areas, the model that best expresses the desirable relationship between mankind and the earth is that spoken of in the following quotations:

> For the Lord shall comfort Zion: he will comfort all her waste places; and he will make her wilderness like Eden, and her desert like the *garden of the Lord*; joy and gladness shall be found therein, thanksgiving, and the voice of melody." (Isaiah 51:3; italics added.)
>
> The designs of God . . . have been to promote the universal good of the universal world; to establish peace and good will among men; to promote the principles of eternal truth; to bring about a state of things that shall unite man to his fellow man; cause the world to "beat their swords into plowshares, and their spears into pruning hooks," make the nations of the earth dwell in peace, and to bring about the millennial glory, when "the earth shall yield her increase," resume its [paradisiacal] glory, and become as *the garden of the Lord.*" (*TPJS,* pp. 248–49; italics added.)

With the above-mentioned caveat, that if we value the future we must maintain essential wilderness areas, humanity's dominion over all the earth is best expressed if we think of the earth as a garden and treat it accordingly. What are the characteristics of a garden that lend themselves to such a line of thought? There are at least five that commend themselves to us, as follows:

1. *Collaboration with nature.* Every gardener knows that to be successful he [or she] must learn to become a collaborator with nature, to form a creative partnership with it. Good gardeners take full advantage of whatever they have going for them in the way of climate, geography, rainfall, soil, and so on, while attempting to minimize the natural disadvantages with which they have to deal. The result is a symbiotic relationship between man and nature that benefits both.

2. *Planning and purpose.* No garden can succeed for long unless the gardener knows what he or she wishes to do and, with that clear

purpose in mind, plans how best to achieve it, without favoring short-term gain at the expense of long-term adverse effects.

3. *Productivity.* A garden, if it is to be successful, must be productive. Similarly, those who have stewardship over "the garden of the Lord," the earth, must work hard to make it productive—to produce the food, fiber, and so on needed by the world's population. That may well require creation of new ecosystems that take advantage of natural possibilities and potentials that would not be exposed were the earth left in a state of wilderness. In fulfilling his stewardship, man has both the right and the responsibility to manage the environment, providing he does so wisely and reverently.

4. *Sustainability and renewal.* Good gardeners spend much time ensuring their garden maintains or even increases its productivity from year to year. They labor to build up the quality of the soil, to protect their crops from insects, wandering deer, and so on, and to introduce improved varieties of plants. They know that failure to do so will lead to decreased productivity in the long run.

5. *Beauty.* Good gardeners strive for that combination of form and color that pleases the eye and fills the heart with delight. They understand the saying of the poet Keats: "A thing of beauty is a joy forever." (*Bartlett's Familiar Quotations*, p. 475.)

Humanity's dominion over the earth would be exalted if all people thought of the earth as a garden and, in their dealings and interaction with it, strove to collaborate with nature, increase productivity, sustain and renew the earth's production capacity, and feed the soul with the beauties and wonder of living things. Truly we could then say that our dwelling place is like Zion.

Every part of the world has lands that have been treated as a garden for very long periods of time, with the desired results mentioned above having been achieved for centuries. China and parts of Europe, for example, have maintained fertile soils and sustained food production for thousands of years through careful management of resources.

Success has been achieved in many regions of the earth not highly favored by nature. I think of the terraced vineyards that rise on steep slopes hundreds of feet above the north end of Lake Geneva in Switzerland. Grapes have been grown there continuously for over 2,000 years. Israel, the biblical land of milk and honey, became largely desert over time as successive generations abused the land and degraded its natural abilities to renew itself. Skillful ecological management, including irrigation and reforestation, now again is causing the desert to "rejoice, and blossom as the rose." (Isaiah 35:1.)

Few places on earth are more pleasing to the eye than is the English countryside, with its hedgerows, meadows, fields, and trees. This admirable landscape is, in effect, a large garden, far different from what it was in the state of wilderness, that has been progressively shaped from the primeval marsh and forest by centuries of effective human intervention. Roadsides and riverbanks have been trimmed and verged with grass; there is a balance between trees and open spaces and between foregrounds and backgrounds. With that aesthetically pleasing balance, achieved through centuries of toil, there has been created a great diversity of ecologic systems. They appear natural to us but in reality owe their origin to human intervention. The hedgerows, for example, with their associated fields, drainage ditches, and lines of trees, date largely from the Enclosure Acts of the seventeenth and eighteenth centuries. (See Asa Briggs, *A Social History of England*, 2nd ed. [London: Pelican Books, 1987], pp. 204–5.) As open fields were enclosed, woodlands and wastes disappeared, and a new pattern of hedges, walls, fences, and rocks took shape. The new plantings and arrangements matured over time and took on the pleasing features so characteristic of today's English countryside. It all looks so natural that it is easy to forget its largely human origin.

The English hedgerows, ditchbanks, and woods harbor an immense variety of plants, insects, songbirds, rodents, and larger mammals, existing together in a pleasing and highly diversified ecosystem, in symbiotic relationship with the humans who dwell there.

In the United States, one of the best examples of treating the earth like a garden is found at Monticello, Thomas Jefferson's Virginia home. "No occupation is so delightful to me as the culture of the earth," wrote Jefferson, "and no culture comparable to that of the garden. . . . But though an old man, I am but a young gardener." The grounds around Monticello became, in Jefferson's hands, a "kind of living laboratory for the study of useful and ornamental plants from around the world."

When Jefferson mentioned his "garden," he was usually referring to his vegetable garden, which "resembled a terraced shelf eighty feet wide and a thousand feet long, cut into the hillside and supported by a stone wall." There, Jefferson grew more than 250 varieties of vegetables and herbs, including sesame, sea kale, tomatoes (then relatively unknown), and "nearly twenty varieties of . . . peas, believed to be his favorite vegetable." ("Thomas Jefferson's Monticello," pamphlet published by the Thomas Jefferson Memorial Foundation, Charlottesville, Virginia.)

It is apparent from the above that the earth is to be seen "neither as an ecosystem to be preserved unchanged nor as a quarry to be exploited for selfish and short-range economic reasons, but as a garden to be cultivated for the development of its own potentialities. . . . The goal of this relationship is not the maintenance of the status quo, but the emergence of new phenomena and new values." (René

Dubois, "Symbiosis Between the Earth and Humankind," *Science*, 193:459–62.)

This view is fully compatible with God's instructions to Adam to replenish the earth, to dress it and keep it. It presupposes the need for work to accomplish the associated stewardship ("In the sweat of thy face shalt thou eat bread" [Genesis 3:19]) and suggests that man, in keeping with his assigned dominion over every living thing, has both the right and the obligation to manage the resources of the earth in ways that will benefit both it and humankind. At the same time, it rejects the "loot and burn" philosophy that has characterized much human interaction with the earth and other living creatures.

RESPONSIBILITIES OF A ZION PEOPLE

If we are, then, to become a Zion people, we must learn well and practice effectively our responsibilities to act as stewards over earthly blessings. Most of us, perhaps, can do little directly about the Brazilian rain forest or global warming. We can, however, do much to control our own micro-environments, acting as good citizens and wise stewards. To do so may be as simple as looking after our own properties in a responsible manner. "We are concerned," said President Kimball, "when we see numerous front and side and back yards that have gone to weeds, when ditch banks are cluttered and trash and refuse accumulate. It grieves us when we see broken fences, falling barns, leaning and unpainted sheds, hanging gates, and unpainted property. And we ask our people again to take stock of their own dwellings and properties.

"There is a story that President Brigham Young, having urged the people of certain communities to properly clear and clean their premises, refused to go back to them to preach to them, saying something like this: 'You didn't listen to me when I urged you to fix up your premises. The same doors are off their hinges; the same barns are still unpainted; the same fences are partly fallen.'" (*Ensign,* May 1975, p. 5.)

"We look forward," concluded President Kimball, "to the day when in all of our communities, urban and rural, there would be a universal, continued movement to clean and repair and paint barns and sheds, build sidewalks, clean ditch banks, and make our properties a thing of beauty to behold." (*Ensign,* November 1974, p. 4.)

As I have traveled in many lands, at home and abroad, I have often thought of President Kimball's wise advice. We must do more! The conclusion seems inescapable: Zion, the pure in heart, is also Zion the clean, Zion the protector of the environment, Zion the faithful steward over earthly blessings.

Chapter Five

"And There Was No Poor among Them"

The scriptures are replete with references to our responsibility to care for the poor and needy and the blessings that will be ours if we do so. "Blessed is he that considereth the poor," sang the Psalmist. "The Lord will deliver him in time of trouble." (Psalm 41:1.) God's interest in the poor and in our attitudes and actions toward them is revealed in this verse from Proverbs: "Whoso mocketh the poor reproacheth his Maker." (Proverbs 17:5.)

Jesus, whose heart was full of compassion for the poor and oppressed, was asked by a young man what was necessary to obtain eternal life. The Savior's reply tells much: "If thou wilt be perfect, go and sell that thou hast, and give to the poor, and thou shalt have treasure in heaven: and come and follow me." (Matthew 19:21.) Matthew records that the young man went away sorrowing, "for he had great possessions." Not for the first (nor, sadly, the last) time, riches had triumphed over righteousness.

The Nephite prophets spoke out boldly against those who "persist in turning [their] backs upon the poor, and the needy, and in withholding [their] substance from them" (Alma 5:55), who "love

money, and . . . substance, and . . . fine apparel, and the adorning of
. . . churches, more than [they] love the poor and the needy"
(Mormon 8:37), and committed all such to damnation "except they
speedily repent" (Alma 5:56).

The responsibility to care for the poor has repeatedly been
emphasized by God's latter-day prophets as well. "And now, I give
unto the church . . . a commandment, that certain men . . . shall be
appointed, . . . and they shall look to the poor and the needy, and
administer to their relief that they shall not suffer." (D&C 38:34–35.)
In the early days of this dispensation, Bishop Newel K. Whitney was
instructed to "travel round about and among all the churches, search-
ing after the poor to administer to their wants." (D&C 84:112.)

Joseph Smith encouraged each member of the Church to serve
others liberally regardless of the receiver's beliefs or church affilia-
tion. The Prophet said: "He [the Church member] is to feed the hungry, to clothe the naked, to provide for the widow, to dry up the tear
of the orphan, to comfort the afflicted, whether in this Church, in any
other, or in no church at all, wherever he finds them." (*Times and
Seasons*, March 15, 1842.) Caring for the poor and needy through
Welfare Services, as President Spencer W. Kimball has indicated, "is
not a program, but the essence of the gospel. It is the gospel in
action. It is the crowning principle of a Christian life." (*Ensign,*
November 1977, p. 77.)

In light of these inspired words, is it any wonder that in the City
of Enoch, where "the Lord called His people Zion, because they
were of one heart and one mind, and dwelt in righteousness; . . .
there was no poor among them"? (Moses 7:18; italics added.) If the
Latter-day Saints are to become a Zion people, we must fully and
completely follow the Lord's admonition to care for the poor. "It is
folly for the Saints to neglect their duties and still think, while doing
so," said President George Q. Cannon, "that within some given

period Zion will be redeemed. Zion will be redeemed, and it may be within the period estimated by them; but they will not be in a position to be benefited by it if they are neglectful and dilatory in seeking for and acquiring that knowledge of the truth which their position and relationship to God and His work admits of their obtaining." (*Gospel Truth* [Salt Lake City: Deseret Book Company, 1987], p. 35.)

Why are we obligated to care for the poor? It is easy to dismiss this question by simply replying, "Because God has so commanded us." While such a reply obviously is true, we may find it instructive to consider briefly some of the reasons *why* God has placed such heavy emphasis on caring for the poor. They include the following, not in any particular order of priority or importance:

1. *We are, literally, brothers and sisters.* Latter-day Saints believe that God is, literally, the Father of the spirits of all humankind. It follows, then, that all men, everywhere, are my brothers, and all women, my sisters. I am tied to each of them by the bonds of kinship. When they bleed, I hurt; when they weep, I mourn. Their pains and sorrows must become mine. I recognize, of course, that these bonds of brotherhood and sisterhood are honored more in the breach than in the observance in the wicked world in which we live, a world in which "man's inhumanity to man makes countless thousands mourn." (Robert Burns, in *Bartlett's Familiar Quotations* [Boston: Little, Brown and Co., 1980], p. 408.) But the principle remains true—a mark of the Zion people of God. Only to the extent that we are willing to "bear one another's burdens, . . . and . . . mourn with those that mourn; . . . and comfort those that stand in need of comfort" (Mosiah 18:8 9) can we ever become a Zion people. Brigham Young, who understood well the kinship of all men and women, said: "We are not isolated and alone, differently formed and composed of different material from the rest of the human race. We

belong to and are part of this family, consequently we are under obligations one to another, and the Latter-day Saints in these mountains are under obligation to their brethren and sisters scattered in the nations who, through indigent circumstances, are unable to gather to themselves the comforts of life." (*Journal of Discourses,* 13:301.)

Concern for our brothers and sisters must go beyond sympathy, or even empathy, to action. "If a brother or sister be naked, and destitute of daily food, and one of you say unto them, Depart in peace, be ye warmed and filled; notwithstanding ye give them not those things which are needful to the body; what doth it profit?" (James 2:15–16.) "The Latter-day Saints have got to learn . . . ," said Brigham Young, "that the interest of their brethren is their own interest, or they never can be saved in the celestial kingdom of God." (*Journal of Discourses,* 3:331.) Prayer and action are inseparable. Faith must lead to works, if it is to become living faith and thus have real meaning in people's lives.

2. *In helping others we find God and save ourselves.* In his farewell address to his people, wise King Benjamin said: "For the sake of retaining a remission of your sins from day to day, that ye may walk guiltless before God—I would that ye should impart of your substance to the poor, every man according to that which he hath, such as feeding the hungry, clothing the naked, visiting the sick and administering to their relief, both spiritually and temporally, according to their wants." (Mosiah 4:26.) The Apostle Paul spoke along similar lines: "Charge them that are rich in this world, that they be not highminded, nor trust in uncertain riches, but in the living God, who giveth us richly all things to enjoy; that they do good, that they be rich in good works, ready to distribute, willing to communicate; laying up in store for themselves a good foundation against the time to come, that they may lay hold on eternal life." (1 Timothy 6:17–19.)

How can caring for the poor, being "rich in good works," help us in "retaining a remission of [our] sins from day to day" and assist us to "lay hold on eternal life"? The answers, I think, lie in the following scriptures:

"When ye are in the service of your fellow beings ye are only in the service of your God." (Mosiah 2:17.)

"Thou shalt worship the Lord thy God, and him only shalt thou serve." (Luke 4:8.)

"Ye have entered into a covenant with him [i.e., the Lord], that ye will serve him and keep his commandments, that he may pour out his Spirit more abundantly upon you." (Mosiah 18:10.)

"There was a time granted unto man to repent, yea, a probationary time, a time to repent and serve God." (Alma 42:4.)

"If thou lovest me thou shalt serve me and keep all my commandments." (D&C 42:29.)

"And remember in all things the poor and the needy, the sick and the afflicted, for he that doth not these things, the same is not my disciple." (D&C 52:40.)

The meaning is clear: We show our love for God, our obedience to Him, our willingness to become a disciple of Christ, as we serve others. A condition for the remission of our sins is that we serve others. In a sense, we are forgiven of our sins to the extent that we care for others and help to ease their burdens. Service is the very essence of godhood; it is synonymous with keeping the commandments of God; it is the offspring of others and thank God for the privilege of being able to do so.

As we recognize that all are beggars, ourselves included, our sense of awareness about the human condition increases. We feel in our hearts the pain and suffering of others, and we weep with them wherever they are. Barriers of geography, language, and culture fall away. Our feelings of gratitude for blessings increases, while at the same time we reach out to help others whom we see, perhaps for the first time, as truly our brothers and sisters. To Cain's cynical and dismissive question "Am I my brother's keeper?" (Genesis 4:9), we reply, "No, but I am his brother, and thus I share in his sorrows and must do all I can to help alleviate them."

3. *The spiritual and temporal are interrelated.* In a general sense, the poor seem to be more sensitive to the whisperings of the Spirit than are the rich. However, Jesus condemns both the poor whose hearts are not broken and whose spirits are not contrite, and the rich who will not give their substance to the poor. (See D&C 56:16–17.) "But blessed are the poor," he said, "who are pure in heart, whose hearts are broken, and whose spirits are contrite, for they shall see the kingdom of God coming in power and great glory unto their deliverance; for the fatness of the earth shall be theirs. For behold, the Lord shall come, and his recompense shall be with him, and he shall reward every man, and the poor shall rejoice; and their generations shall inherit the earth from generation to generation, forever and ever." (Vv. 18–20.)

Poverty is a relative thing and difficult to define precisely. It means something different in Nigeria than in the United States. Yet there is a state of want and misery below which no one should be asked to descend so long as others live in plenty. Those of us with many blessings must learn to live simply so that others may simply live. Remember, "a religion that has not the power to save people temporally . . . cannot be depended upon to save them spiritually." (President Joseph F. Smith, quoted in Albert E. Bowen, *The Church Welfare Plan*, Sunday School Gospel Doctrine Course, 1946, p. 36.)

Men, women, and children simply cannot develop their spiritual faculties if the material conditions for their existence reduce them to the level of animal survival. It is said that for many people there is no morality below 900 calories of food energy per day. Under such conditions of want and deprivation, many will do whatever is necessary to survive, even if that means breaking God's commandments. It does little good to speak of spiritual things to one whose children are dying from hunger. While counseling those who would welcome the survivors of the Willie and Martin handcart companies to the Salt Lake Valley, Brigham Young said: "You know that I would give more for a dish of pudding and milk, or a baked potato and salt, were I in the situation of those persons who have just come in, than I would for all your prayers, though you were to stay here all the afternoon and pray. Prayer is good, but when baked potatoes and pudding and milk are needed, prayer will not supply their place." (*Deseret News Weekly*, 6 [December 10, 1856]: 320.)

"I want to say to you," said President Harold B. Lee, "that we might just as well throw our hats in the air and scream as to hope to convert spiritually an individual family or an individual man or an individual nation whose existence has been reduced to the instincts of animal survival. . . . We must take care of their material needs and give them a taste of the kind of salvation that they do not have to die to get before we can lift their thinking to a higher plane." (General Welfare Meeting, April 4, 1959.)

In other words, needy people may require material assistance as a prerequisite to teaching them the higher spiritual truths. The spiritual and temporal parts of our existence cannot be separated.

THE EXTENT OF POVERTY IN THE WORLD

Poverty exists in every nation and in every community. In its extreme manifestations, it is a form of bondage and the root cause of many social ills. Disease, malnutrition, crime, and illiteracy are in a general sense at much higher levels among those who live in countries with low gross national products than in those where the gross national product is significantly higher.

The following data, produced by the World Bank, illustrate some of the relationships involved for selected low-, middle-, and high-income countries.

VITAL STATISTICS IN 18 SELECTED COUNTRIES

Country	G.N.P * $ per capita 1989	Life expectancy Years 1989	%Adult Illiteracy 1985	Infant mortality 1000 live births 1989
Low Income Countries				
Mozambique	80	49	62	137
Somalia	170	48	88	128
Nigeria	250	51	58	100
Haiti	360	55	62	94
Ghana	390	55	40	86
Middle Income Countries				
Bolivia	620	54	26	106
Philippines	710	64	14	42
Dom. Rep.	790	67	23	61
Colombia	1,200	69	12	38
Mexico	2,010	69	10	40
High Income Countries				
Spain	9,330	77	6	8
Australia	14,360	77	Neg.**	8
U. K.	14,610	76	Neg.	9
Canada	19,030	77	Neg.	7
United States	20,910	76	Neg.	10

* = Gross National Product
** = Negligible—i.e. less than 5%
(*World Development Report*, 1991, The World Bank, Oxford University Press, Tables 1 and 28.)

Average income levels, as measured by gross national product per capita, vary widely—from less than 100 U.S. dollars per year to over 20,000 U.S. dollars per year. Indeed, there are thirty-two countries with G.N.P.'s per capita of less than 500 U.S. dollars per year, twenty-three of them in Africa. Life expectancy in low-income countries such as Somalia or Nigeria is more than twenty-five years less than in high-income countries such as Canada or the United States. Adult illiteracy rates are ten to fifteen times higher in low-income countries than in high-income, developed Western countries. The figures shown are for both men and women. In *every* instance, illiteracy rates are higher for adult women than for adult men. In fact, fewer than 15 percent of women in Black Africa are literate. In the absence of literacy, it is difficult to raise health, nutritional, and sanitary standards. Illiterate people have a difficult time improving their living standards, reading the sacred scriptures, and understanding and acting on their options, truly using their moral agency.

Infant mortality rates in low-income countries are fifteen to twenty times higher than in developed countries. It is noteworthy that U.S. rates (10 per 1,000 live births) are considerably higher than those in other developed countries such as Canada (7) or Sweden (6).

THE IRISH POTATO FAMINE

The effects of poverty and its consequences on a population are well illustrated by the sad story of the potato famine that decimated Ireland in the nineteenth century. In the early 1840s, Ireland had a population of more than eight million, twice what it has today. The Irish peasantry lived in abject poverty. Said the Duke of Wellington, himself an Irishman, "There never was a country in which poverty existed to the extent it exists in Ireland." "Housing conditions were wretched beyond words. . . . Nearly half of the families of the rural population [were] living [in] windowless mud cabins of a single room. . . . Furniture was a luxury; the inhabitants of Tullahobagly,

County Donegal, numbering about 9,000, had in 1837 only 10 beds, 93 chairs and 243 stools between them." (*The Great Hunger*, Cecil Woodham-Smith [New York: Harper & Row, 1962], p. 20.)

The diet of most Irish people consisted almost entirely of potatoes; a staggering average of fourteen pounds per person were consumed each day. Disaster struck in August of 1845 when initial reports began to appear of disease in the potato crop. Within a few weeks, most of the crop was infected and destroyed. In 1846 and again in 1848, the crop failed completely. Even potatoes that seemed healthy when dug began to rot in storage and soon were unfit to eat.

There was no other locally produced food to which the people could turn for sustenance, and almost nobody had any money to pay for anything anyway. Despair and foreboding hung like a dark cloud over the island. Such grain as was grown was used largely to pay rents, almost always to absentee landlords in England. Unlike their English counterparts, Irish farmers had no rights of tenancy secured by law. Any improvements they made on the land only put Irishmen at risk of increased rents or even eviction.

By October of 1845, famine was beginning to appear, and disaster loomed. A young English medical officer sent to Ireland wrote, "Famine must be looked forward to and there will follow, as a natural consequence, as in former years, typhus fever or some other malignant pestilence." His gloomy prophecy was soon proven correct. (Richard M. Krause, *The Restless Tide* [Washington, D.C.: National Foundation for Infectious Diseases, 1981], p. 52.)

The British government, committed to the principles of laissez-faire economics which forbade any interference with market forces, refused to intervene. The Irish would just have to feed themselves with their own resources. During 1846 and 1847, there was no government relief, no government buying of food; and the costs of public works, the only form of relief, had to be borne entirely from local taxes. That in itself ensured that little was done.

The Irish economy simply could not respond effectively. Even in good times Ireland imported almost nothing. There were few roads, especially in the remote western parts of the island; and only rudimentary systems of food distribution existed. On top of that, as already noted, the Irish peasantry were the poorest and most ignorant in all of Europe.

People by the millions soon were reduced to living on nettles, roots, seaweed, even grass. It was not long before they began to die from malnutrition and the infectious diseases that invariably follow it, primarily typhus and relapsing fever. In February 1847, a Royal Navy captain who visited Schull, a seaboard village in County Cork, reported that it "was half derelict, and most of the people were in the last stages of starvation. Some were like living skeletons"; others had "bodies swollen to twice their normal size," their skins blotched and blackened by scurvy. "Here and there corpses lay on the ground." (*Heaven's Command*, James Morris [London: Penguin Books, 1973], pp. 152–53.) The horror of Schull was repeated throughout the whole of Ireland.

The total of those who died will never be known, although a figure of between 1 and 1.5 million is commonly used. Probably ten times as many died from disease as from malnutrition.

By 1848, the British government, acting against all its avowed principles, decided finally to make some relief available. A soup of sorts was provided to feed the poor. Scarcely more nutritious than hot water, the recipe intended to feed 100 men consisted of 1/4 pound of beef leg, 2 ounces of dripping, 2 onions, 1/2 pound of flour, 1/2 pound of pearl barley, 3 ounces of salt, and 1/2 ounce of brown sugar, in two gallons of water. (Ibid., p. 166)

But it was too little too late; Ireland was ruined, its people broken in body and spirit. By the hundreds of thousands the desperate survivors fled, most to the United States via Canada. Those coming to Canada arrived weak, sick, and dying at the quarantine station of Grosse Isle on the Saint Lawrence River below Quebec City. Many failed in their desperate diaspora and are buried on Grosse Isle; a monument there commemorates their misery. "In this secluded spot," it reads, "lie the mortal remains of 5,424 persons who flying from pestilence and famine in Ireland in the year 1847 found in America but a grave." (Ibid., p. 174.)

The story of the Irish potato famine is a classic case study of poverty, disease, indifference, and ignorance—a tragic example of how not to care for the poor. (For additional details on the Irish potato famine, see *Heaven's Command,* the first volume of James Morris's magnificent trilogy on the British Empire [London: Penguin Books, 1973], pp. 152–74; *Eyewitness to History*, John Carey ed. [New York: Avon Books, 1987], p. 320; and Cecil Woodham-Smith, *The Great Hunger* [New York: Harper & Row, 1962].)

CARING FOR THE POOR IN THE LORD'S WAY

How, then, are we to care for the poor in ways that will best help them? Frankly, we cannot look to worldly models for an example of what should be done (though they tell us much about what should not be done) but must look elsewhere. The Lord has made it clear that "it is [His] purpose to provide for [His] Saints" (D&C 104:15), but He adds, "It must needs be done in mine own way; and behold this is the way that I, the Lord, have decreed to provide for my saints, that the poor shall be exalted, in that the rich are made low" (D&C 104:16).

What does it mean to exalt the poor and make the rich low? The rich are made low as they humble themselves, giving freely of that which they have to those in need, recognizing that all earthly blessings come from God. The poor are exalted as they receive help with gratitude, with hearts that are pure and broken and spirits that are contrite. The help they receive releases them from the bondage under which they labor and enables them to rise to their full potential temporally and spiritually by becoming self-reliant. Then they are able and willing to reach out to help others. As the rich are humbled and the poor exalted, both are sanctified, or made holy, taking on the characteristics of a Zion people.

Caring for the poor in the Lord's way is not an easy thing to do; achieving the necessary balance between giving too much and giving too little is one of the most difficult tasks priesthood leaders and others have to carry out. Each situation is different, requiring its own solution. All the poor are not the same. Brigham Young, with perhaps unintentional wry humor, noted that there are three classes of the poor: "the Lord's poor, the devil's poor, and the poor devils." (*Journal of Discourses,* 12:57.) Some are poor in economic terms; others are poor in spirit, depressed, disheartened, burdened with cares and sorrow, perhaps disabled. Among them are the aged, the widow, the single mother. All need compassion; all merit our concern.

Unless tempered by good judgment, however, compassion may lead to failure unless basic principles associated with success are followed. These principles include the following:

Love. No program, system, or process of caring for the poor will succeed unless it is based upon love. The love of God and of His children are inseparably connected: "Thou shalt love the Lord thy God with all thy heart, and with all thy soul, and with all thy mind. This is the first and great commandment. And the second is like unto it, thou shalt love thy neighbour as thyself." (Matthew 22:37–39.) John goes to the heart of the matter with this question: "But whoso hath this world's good, and seeth his brother have need, and shutteth up his bowels of compassion from him, how dwelleth the love of God in him?" (1 John 3:17.) Love lies at the root of God's plan for caring for the poor.

Although nothing could have been done to prevent the occurrence of potato blight in Ireland a century and a half ago, the response to the ensuing crisis was conditioned by attitudes in England toward the Irish people. The quarrels and misunderstandings between the two countries were, even in the nineteenth century, seven hundred years old. No love was lost on either side. Little wonder, then, that efforts to reduce the burden of famine on the people were marked by indifference and misunderstanding.

Work. "Thou shalt not be idle," the Lord has said, "for he that is idle shall not eat the bread nor wear the garments of the laborer." (D&C 42:42.) To our father Adam, He proclaimed, "In the sweat of thy face shalt thou eat bread." (Genesis 3:19.) Work is the prerequisite for self-respect and self-reliance. It does away with the curse of idleness and the evils of the dole. "The aim of the Church," said the First Presidency in 1936, "is to help the people to help themselves. Work is to be re-enthroned as the ruling principle of the lives of our Church membership." (*Conference Report,* October 1936, p. 3.) Those who, out of a misguided compassion, provide for others without giving them an opportunity to work for what they get will in the long run produce a soul-threatening dependence. "It is not an unkind or an unfeeling bishop who requires a member to work to the fullest extent he can for what he receives from Church welfare," Elder Boyd K. Packer pointed out in a stirring General Conference address a few years ago. (*Ensign,* May 1978, p. 91.)

"My experience has taught me," said Brigham Young, "and it has become a principle with me, that it is never any benefit to give, out and out, to man or woman, money, food, clothing, or anything else, if they are able-bodied, and can work and earn what they need, when there is anything on the earth for them to do. This is my principle, and I try to act upon it. To pursue a contrary course would ruin any community in the world and make them idlers." (*Journal of Discourses,* 11:297.) "Set the poor to work—setting out orchards, splitting rails, digging ditches, making fences, or anything useful, and so enable them to buy meal and flour and the necessaries of life." (*Journal of Discourses,* 12:61.)

During the Irish potato famine, with some laudable exceptions, little was done by the authorities to provide work to those in want. Indeed, by the beginning of 1848, nearly half a million men in Ireland had no work at all! As already indicated, to be without work is a great curse, not a blessing. It destroys men and women, crushing the self-respect out of them. I recall a song of my youth called "The Big Rock Candy Mountain." It told of a place where no effort was needed, where anything one wanted could be picked up from the ground or off the trees, where "the bulldogs all have rubber teeth and the hens lay soft-boiled eggs." In the Big Rock Candy Mountain "you don't need any money." To a small boy the line "In the Big Rock Candy Mountain, you never change your socks" seemed particularly alluring! I now realize that the Big Rock Candy Mountain of song and legend is not a desirable place to be. Without work, without sweat and effort, there can be no happiness and no spiritual progression.

A pamphlet relative to the Church Welfare Program, "Helping Others to Help Themselves," first published about 1945, points out the trials that come to those who have no work:

> A man out of work is of special moment to the Church because, deprived of his inheritance, he is on trial as Job was on trial—for his integrity.
>
> As days lengthen into weeks and months and even years of

adversity, the hurt grows deeper, and he is sorely tempted to "curse God and die."

Continued economic dependence breaks him, it humiliates him if he is strong, spoils him if he is weak. Sensitive or calloused, despondent or indifferent, rebellious or resigned—either way, he is threatened with spiritual ruin, for the dole is an evil and idleness a curse.

He soon becomes the seedbed of discontent, wrong thinking, alien beliefs. The Church cannot hope to save a man on Sunday if during the week it is a complacent witness to the crucifixion of his soul.

Self-Reliance. "No amount of philosophizing, excuses, or rationalizing will ever change the fundamental need for self-reliance," said President Spencer W. Kimball (*Ensign,* May 1978, p. 79). Indeed, from the beginning of time, mortals have been counseled by God and His prophets to be self-reliant, to earn their own way, to be independent, and to avoid temporal or spiritual bondage. Such bondage may range from an attitude that "the world owes me a living" to drug or alcohol dependency, unwise debt, or the spiritual bondage of sin. Bondage may arise from excessive dependency on others, including ecclesiastical leaders. Those who are so bound expect others to make moral and spiritual decisions for them. Sometimes, as Elder Boyd K. Packer has wisely pointed out, bishops and other leaders become unwitting accomplices in establishing and maintaining that dependency. He said:

> Bishops, keep constantly in mind that fathers are responsible to preside over their families.
>
> Sometimes, with all good intentions, we require so much of both the children and the father that he is not able to do so.
>
> If my boy needs counseling, bishop, it should be my responsibility first, and yours second.
>
> If my boy needs recreation, bishop, I should provide it first, and you second.

If my boy needs correction, that should be my responsibility first, and yours second.

If I am failing as a father, help me first, and my children second.

Do not be too quick to take over from me the job of raising my children.

Do not be too quick to counsel them and solve all of the problems. Get me involved. It is my ministry. (*Ensign*, May 1978, p. 93.)

Why is it that God places such emphasis on the principle of self-reliance? The answer becomes clear when we understand that self-reliance is closely tied to freedom.

The scriptures are clear in telling us that freedom is a God-given principle of life. Samuel the Lamanite proclaimed: "Behold, ye are free; ye are permitted to act for yourselves; for behold, God hath given unto you a knowledge and he hath made you free." (Helaman 14:30.) We cannot be free if we are not self-reliant. Put another way, self-reliance is a prerequisite for freedom, and dependence is the enemy of freedom. The scriptures (D&C 29:24–35) tell us that man is intended by God to be "an agent unto himself." He cannot do so unless he is self-reliant. Independence and self-reliance thus are critical keys to spiritual growth. Whenever we are in a situation that threatens self-reliance, we will find that freedom is threatened too.

Although self-reliance and freedom are tied together, there is nothing spiritual, in and of itself, in being self-reliant. In our laudable strivings to attain self-reliance, we must be careful not to rely too much on the arm of flesh and to remember that we are wholly reliant upon God for all of life's blessings, including life itself. One could be self-reliant—completely independent—and lack every other desirable attribute of character. I think of a man who was one of the most wealthy men in the world, an American oil baron. He is dead now, but while he lived, a more miserable soul would have been hard to find. Grasping, conniving, greedy, incapable of giving, concerned only with getting, his wealth had cankered his soul. His self-reliance did him no good. Self-reliant does not mean self-centered!

Self-reliance, then, is not an end but a means to an end. Self-reliance becomes a factor in spiritual growth only as we use the freedom it brings to make the right choices. In particular, those who are self-reliant are free to serve others. The Nephite prophet Jacob said, "Think of your brethren like unto yourselves, and be familiar with all and free with your substance, that they may be rich like unto you. But before ye seek for riches, seek ye for the kingdom of God. And after ye have obtained a hope in Christ ye shall obtain riches, if ye seek them; and ye will seek them for the intent to do good—to clothe the naked, and to feed the hungry, and to liberate the captive, and administer relief to the sick and the afflicted." (Jacob 2:17–19.) In other words, we are to use earthly resources to serve others.

Service is linked to sacrifice. It is through sacrifice that we become sanctified and purified. I think of a family in the Liverpool England Stake, in whose home I visited a few years ago. A child in the home had been born with a rare metabolic disease that prevented her from growing and developing normally. Though she was eight years old when I saw her, the poor little thing weighed only about twenty pounds. Bedridden, still an infant, she cried in pain every few minutes. Her devoted mother tenderly cared for the youngster day and night and had not enjoyed an uninterrupted night's sleep since the child's birth. The mother was always there, easing her child's pain, whatever the hour. In the process of sharing and enduring suffering, that good woman had become sanctified. Her face was that of an angel of mercy. The purity of her soul was apparent to all. She had become a handmaiden of the Lord, united with Him in her work of mercy and love.

Unity. President J. Reuben Clark preached often upon the theme of unity, using as his scriptural basis the following verse: "I say unto you, be one; and if ye are not one ye are not mine." (D&C 38:27.) Unity is indeed one of the central themes of the gospel, expressed in its perfection in the unity between Jesus and his apostles at the Last Supper. (See John 17:20–21.) Significantly, the people of Enoch were of "one heart and one mind" (Moses 7:18), and in the Nephite Zion there were no contentions among the people. (See 4 Nephi 1:13.)

Brigham Young spoke often about the importance of unity. "We have come here to build up Zion," he said. "How shall we do it? . . . . I have told you a great many times. There is one thing I will say in regard to it. We have got to be united in our efforts. We should go to work with a united faith like the heart of one man; and whatever we do should be performed in the name of the Lord, and we will then be blessed and prospered in all we do." (*Journal of Discourses,* 13:155.)

Significantly, as the time of dedication of the Salt Lake Temple drew near, the First Presidency (Wilford Woodruff, George Q. Cannon, and Joseph F. Smith) sent the following message to the Saints:

> We feel now that a time for reconciliation has come; that before entering into the Temple to present ourselves before the Lord in solemn assembly, we shall divest ourselves of every harsh and unkind feeling against each other; that not only our bickerings shall cease, but that the cause of them shall be removed, and every sentiment that prompted and maintained them shall be dispelled; that we shall confess our sins one to another, and ask forgiveness one of another; that we shall plead with the Lord for the spirit of repentance, and having obtained it, follow its promptings; so that in humbling ourselves before Him and seeking forgiveness from each other, we shall yield that charity and generosity to those who crave our forgiveness that we ask for and expect from Heaven.

Thus may we come up into the holy place with our hearts free
from guile and our souls prepared for the edification that is
promised! Thus shall our supplications, undisturbed by a thought
of discord, unitedly mount into the ears of Jehovah and draw down
the choice blessings of the God of Heaven! (*Messages of the First
Presidency* [Salt Lake City: Bookcraft, 1966], 3:243.)

Other American pioneers also understood the importance of
unity. In 1630, John Winthrop, later the first governor of
Massachusetts, read the following message to fellow Puritans aboard
the *Arabella* on their voyage to what has evolved into the United
States of America: "We must be knit together in this work as one.
. . . We must delight in each other; make others' conditions our own;
rejoice together, mourn together, labor and suffer together . . . as
members of the same body." (Robert C. Winthrop, *Life and Letters of
John Winthrop,* 3rd ed. [Boston: Little, Brown and Company, 1895],
2:18–19.)

In the building up of Zion, unity comes from following the light
from above, in learning the will of the Lord and then doing it. The
power of the Church to do good depends upon that principle. We can
accomplish all that God asks of us if we are united. Then will we
become one with Him; then will all of our labor be consecrated to
the salvation of His children and the establishment of the kingdom
of God upon the earth. Those who are unified are repentant and
humble. Their hearts are full of forgiveness, charity, and generosity
toward others.

Caring for the poor and needy "in the Lord's way" can come
about only if we "make others' conditions our own" and labor,
endure, and suffer together. Givers then will be united with receivers,
and the efforts of the givers will be magnified because they are
united to each other. What a glorious principle is unity! It is a hall-
mark of the Zion people of God.

Sanctification. Caring for the poor and needy through selfless service to others produces sanctification, the process by which sin is purged from the soul and one loses "every desire for sin." (*TPJS*, p. 51.) The blood of Christ sanctifies repentant suppliants, cleansing them through His infinite care: "For by the water ye keep the commandment; by the Spirit ye are justified, and by the blood ye are sanctified." (Moses 6:60.) The power of the Holy Ghost enhances the sanctification process; it purifies the heart and confers upon its recipients an inability to "look upon sin save it were with abhorrence." (Alma 13:12.) Those who are thus strengthened go on in humility and faith, yielding their hearts to God and serving others, becoming sanctified, having "no more disposition to do evil, but to do good continually." (Mosiah 5:2.)

One of the humble, unsung heroes of this dispensation, Brother Joseph Millett, portrays the deeds and blessings of those whose hearts are pure, who have been sanctified through service. During those early, difficult pioneer years in the Great Basin, Brother Millett wrote in his journal:

> One of my children came in said that Brother Newton Halls folks was out of bread Had none that day.
> I . . . [divided] our flour in sack to send up to Brother Halls. Just then Brother Hall came in.
> Ses I, Brother Hall how are you out for flour?
> Brother Millett, we have non, well Brother Hall there is some in that sack I have divided and was a going to send it to you your children told mine that you was out.
> Bro Hall began to cry said he had tryed others could not get any Went to the cedars and prayed to the Lord and the Lord told him to go to Joseph Millett.
> Well Brother Hall you needent bring this back if the Lord sent you for it, you dont owe me for it.

That night, humble, sanctified Joseph Millett recorded the following in his journal: "You can't tell how good it made me feel to know that the Lord knew that there was such a person as Joseph Millett." (Joseph Millett Jr. Record Book, p. 88–89, microfilm of manuscript [Salt Lake City: Church Historical Department], pp. 88–89.)

No act of kindness better sanctifies a soul or exemplifies our love for the needy than the giving of a generous fast offering. Those who are niggardly in their giving will wither their souls, while those who are generous move toward the celestial goal of sanctification. President Kimball reminded us of our obligations relative to the law of the fast:

> Each member should contribute a generous fast offering for the care of the poor and the needy. This offering should at least be the value of the two meals not eaten while fasting.
>
> Sometimes we have been a bit penurious and figured that we had for breakfast one egg and that cost so many cents and then we give that to the Lord. I think that when we are affluent, as many of us are, that we ought to be very, very generous. . . .
>
> I think we should . . . give, instead of the amount saved by our two meals of fasting, perhaps much, much more—ten times more when we are in a position to do it. (*Conference Report,* October 1974, p. 184.)

When we, through our efforts to bless and share with those in greater need, master our own desires and wants, "then the powers of the gospel are released in [our] lives. . . . [and we] insure not only temporal salvation but also spiritual sanctification. . . . In the true Zion—one may partake of both temporal and spiritual salvation." (Spencer W. Kimball, *Ensign,* November 1977, p. 77.)

Chapter Six

"A Peculiar Treasure unto Me"

To former-day Israel in the wilderness of Sinai, the Lord declared: "If ye will obey my voice indeed, and keep my covenant, then ye shall be a peculiar treasure unto me above all people: for all the earth is mine: and ye shall be unto me a kingdom of priests, and an holy nation." (Exodus 19:5–6.) In this passage, the Hebrew word for "peculiar" (*segullah*) means "special possession or property." Spiritually speaking, then, Israel, or Zion, is to be a special possession or treasure unto God, a treasure purchased through the atonement of Christ. (See Acts 20:28; 1 Peter 1:18–19.)

The Almighty has laid down two conditions that must be met if the Latter-day Saints are to become a special treasure unto God and a Zion people: We must obey His voice in all things, and we must keep His covenants, as have the Zion societies of the past. Then will we "increase in beauty, and in holiness" (D&C 82:14); "put on [our] strength" (Isaiah 52:1); become "the perfection of beauty" (Psalm 50:2); "[dwell] in righteousness" (Moses 7:18); be called "the city of righteousness, the faithful city" (Isaiah 1:26); and "be redeemed with judgment" (Isaiah 1:27).

Clearly the reason Zion has not been redeemed is that neither of the two required conditions has been met. Although the Lord has said He is well pleased with the Church, speaking collectively and not individually (see D&C 1:30), it is apparent we still have much to do before we become a people worthy of the appellation "Zion."

THE COVENANT PEOPLE OF THE LORD

In the early days of this dispensation, the Saints were sustained in their suffering and persecution by the deep conviction that they were the covenant people of God who had entered into a special relationship with Him. That conviction gave force and impetus to the gathering of the Saints from many lands. They came to the Great Basin, many under conditions of severe hardship, to build up Zion, imbued with the vision that they were a chosen people who had been called by God out of all the nations of the world and had been entrusted with sacred, precious knowledge. President Brigham Young said:

> The Christian world have very limited ideas with regard to the Kingdom of Heaven on the earth. We as Latter-day Saints have confessed before Heaven, before the heavenly hosts, and before the inhabitants of the earth, that we really believe the Scriptures as they are given to us according to the best understanding and knowledge that we have of the translation, and the spirit and meaning of the Old and New Testaments.
>
> We have confessed before angels and men, and have acknowledged by our acts that we believe most assuredly that Jesus has called upon us as his disciples—those who will receive the truth, obey His commandments, observe His precepts and honor His laws, to come out from among the wicked, to separate ourselves from sinners and from sin. If we have not confessed this by our acts as well as by our faith, then we are mistaken concerning the gathering of ourselves together. But we have confessed it, and we do believe it, and it is for us to live according to that which we

acknowledge. We acknowledge the covenant under which we live; we believe it, and are honest in our belief; and we will honor that covenant by obedience to the laws of God. If we do not, our words and our actions contradict each other. By our acts, by our coming together, by our leaving our homes, our friends and our birthplaces that were dear to us according to the customs and belief of the world, we have declared our desire to serve the Lord. (*Journal of Discourses,* 12:227.)

John Murdock, for example, sought for years for a society where the true ordinances of the gospel could be found. He eventually received the witness of the Spirit that the restored gospel preached by Mormon missionaries and found in the Book of Mormon was true. He came to realize that the authority to administer the ordinances of salvation resided in The Church of Jesus Christ of Latter-day Saints. Soon afterward he was baptized. In his autobiography he recorded, "I never before felt the authority of the Ordinance [of baptism], but I felt it this time and felt as though my sins were forgiven." (In Roger R. Keller, "Prepared for the Fulness," *Ensign,* January 1993, p. 23.)

Although the gathering provided a place for mutual protection and spiritual reinforcement, its basic purpose, the Prophet Joseph Smith averred, was to "build unto the Lord a house whereby he could reveal unto his people the ordinances of his house and the glories of his kingdom, and teach the people the way of salvation; for there are certain ordinances and principles that, when they are taught and practiced, must be done in a place or house built for that purpose." (*TPJS,* p. 308.) Significantly, it is in the holy temple that the highest and holiest covenants between God and man are made. Out of His love for us, God provides the temple so that therein we may partake of the covenants that are necessary for us to become a peculiar treasure unto Him.

The concept of a covenant people is of less vital force and has less impact in the lives of many Church members today than in the past. Perhaps we preach and teach about it less frequently than previously. Perhaps some members, anxious to be accepted by others not of our faith, downplay our differences while striving to find common ground with others. Finding and building upon common ground with others is a noble goal if in doing so we do not weaken, dilute, give away, or paper over our doctrine. After all, either the Latter-day Saints, speaking collectively, are the covenant people of the Lord or we are not; and if we are, others are not, at least in the full sense of the term. To say so is not to deride the teachings or beliefs of others nor to assert that they are totally in error or deny them the right to their beliefs. Nor is it to suggest that others do not make some covenants with God. It does not give us license to act as though we are superior to them. It is simply to proclaim that The Church of Jesus Christ of Latter-day Saints has a unique role and responsibility. Ours is a different vision. We have a higher responsibility that calls upon the Church to "stand independent above all other creatures beneath the celestial world." (D&C 78:14.) When properly honored, the covenants we as Latter-day Saints make, perhaps particularly in the temple, have the potential to change the recipients thereof in ways different from those experienced by others not of our faith.

After reciting a list of the covenants made by the Latter-day Saints, President Joseph F. Smith went on to share this about the role of Church members:

> It is expected that [the] officers and presiding authorities in the Church . . . shall see to it that the members of the Church of Jesus Christ of Latter-day Saints will keep these covenants that they have made with the Lord, and that they will observe these principles and adapt them to their lives and carry them out, that they may be indeed the salt of the earth; not salt that has lost its savor

and is good for nothing but to be cast out and trodden under the foot of men, but salt that has its savor and that is wholesome; that the people of God may be a light unto this generation and unto the world; that men may see your good works and glorify your Father which is in heaven; and that notwithstanding enemies, who are filled with the spirit of persecution, and who say all manner of false things against the Latter-day Saints, those who have entered into the covenant of the Gospel will keep the commandments of the Lord, will obey the dictates of the Spirit of the Lord unto them, will work righteousness in the earth, and will go right on in the path that Almighty God has marked out for them to pursue, fulfilling and accomplishing His will and His purposes concerning them in the latter day. (*Conference Report,* October 1904, pp. 4–5.)

What an awesome responsibility falls upon leaders to encourage the members of the Church to keep the covenants! Similarly, what responsibility falls on the members to be a light unto the world and the salt of the earth. Zion can be built up only by the covenant people of God, those who are "a peculiar treasure unto [Him] above all people." The concept of a covenant people is powerfully motivational. It can inspire and lift us up to embrace a more glorious vision of what we may become. It can fill us with the endowment of power that we require to become a sanctified people of Zion, "that as God's people, under His direction and obedient to His law, we may grow up in righteousness and truth; that when His purposes shall be accomplished, we may receive an inheritance among those that are sanctified." (*TPJS,* p. 254.)

The lesson that people respond positively when challenged to greatness is well illustrated by the following tale. Early in this century, so the story goes, the following classified ad appeared in the *Times* of London: "Men wanted for hazardous journey. Low wages, bitter cold, long hours of complete darkness. Safe return doubtful.

Honor and recognition in the event of success." The ad was signed "E. Shackleton." Ernest Shackleton was seeking men to accompany him on his Antarctic explorations. The next morning, more than five thousand men were waiting outside the *Times'* offices! (*Success,* January/February 1993, p. 18.)

Those who take seriously the covenants they make, who aspire to be numbered among the covenant people of God, wish only to be humble disciples of Jesus. They endeavor—whatever their age—to become as little children, "submissive, meek, humble, patient, full of love." (Mosiah 3:19.) They recognize their dependence on God and His goodness. They are not puffed up with a sense of their own importance, knowing that "God resisteth the proud, but giveth grace unto the humble." (James 4:6.) They "love not the world, neither the things that are in the world." (1 John 2:15.) They are called out of the world to become a Zion people in anticipation of the coming of the Savior. They voluntarily accept covenants that require both sacrifice and consecration. They become endowed with the two great attributes that encompass much of the teachings of Jesus: integrity and love.

INTEGRITY

Those who have integrity are whole and complete. They know who they are and who God is. Sincerity, humility, and meekness are part of their character. They are less concerned about being recognized than in being right. They are driven by conscience, not by a desire for credit. "When the issues are determined," said President Marion G. Romney, "whether we stand with the winners or the losers, of this we may be sure: To make the proper choice on any issue is of far more importance to us personally than is the immediate outcome of the issue upon which we make a decision. The choices we make will affect the scope of our agency in the future. As of now, we have the right of decision. What we will have tomorrow depends upon how we decide today." (*Conference Report,* October 1968, p. 68.)

President N. Eldon Tanner was known throughout much of his adult life as "Mister Integrity." As Minister in the Government of Alberta, private businessman, and Church leader, he exemplified the highest ideals of honesty, honor, and superior character, "a man to match our mountains: tall, rugged, unyielding, immoveable," as President Kimball said of his beloved associate. (*Church News,* April 1, 1978, p. 6.) On one occasion, while in government service in Canada, Brother Tanner stood to vote against his own party on a proposal he could not accept. Warned by colleagues that his vote could cost him his government post, Brother Tanner replied, "I would rather be *out* honorably than to be *in* voting against my principles." (G. Homer Durham, *N. Eldon Tanner, His Life and Service* [Salt Lake City: Deseret Book Company, 1982], p. 106.)

When Brother Tanner retired from government service, a newspaper article of the time commented, "The oilmen with whom Tanner has worked in the past five years deeply respect him; they call him a 'hard apple' in tribute to the way in which he has operated his department to squeeze out the most profit for Alberta but still keep the development capital flowing in." (Ibid., p. 108.) Another newspaper editorial read, "For the general good sense of the government's oil policies, most of the credit must go to Hon. Nathan Tanner, whose impending resignation from the cabinet will be received everywhere with genuine regret. . . . We have not always agreed with him, but we respect him; and now on his departure, we sincerely wish him well." (Ibid., p. 107.)

At a banquet in his honor, in response to the tributes paid him, Brother Tanner spoke with characteristic modesty and simplicity of the philosophy that guided his life: "The service we give is the price we pay for the privilege of living in this world. The type of service we give will determine the kind of world we live in." (Ibid., p. 108.) If integrity is the first step to true greatness, President Tanner was well on the way!

An important component of integrity is honesty. When I think of honesty, my thoughts turn to the example set by an American who served his country as an artilleryman in World War I. After the war, he and a partner established a men's clothing store in Kansas City. At first the store prospered, but in the postwar depression of 1921, the two partners fell on hard times. The business failed in 1922, approximately $35,000 in the red. One of the partners filed for bankruptcy, but the other would not. He resolved to pay off his creditors as best he could, little by little. Fifteen years after the store went under, he was still paying business debts and was generally strapped for money for twenty years. But he knew where his duty lay. In later years he did rather well for himself. His name, of course, was Harry S Truman, the thirty-third president of the United States. (David McCullough, *Truman* [New York: Simon and Schuster, 1992], pp. 145–51.) Significantly, on President Truman's desk was a sign, "The Buck Stops Here."

How glorious and pure are those who have integrity! They can sleep at night, secure in the knowledge that they have done their best; their conscience is clear of offense to anyone, their honor unsullied by the sordid compromises and shady dealings of the world. Their values and convictions are clearly defined and well known to their associates. They seek first the kingdom of God and His righteousness and are little interested in power or wealth. They understand that "a man's life consisteth not in the abundance of the things which he possesseth." (Luke 12:15.) They love people and are deeply interested in them. Others see them as people who can be trusted.

Several years ago, a friend of mine who was serving at the time as a stake president, was out of work. He struggled hard to find employment, without success. Part of the problem was that he was nearly fifty years old, and many potential employers turned him down as qualified but too old. After several fruitless months, job interviews fell away to zero. After nearly a year out of work, the family's savings were exhausted and their year's supply of food and other essentials was nearly all used up. My friend was desperate; his self-confidence had eroded to the vanishing point. Finally, he got another job interview. It went well, but the interviewer was undecided, influenced as others had been by my friend's age. Finally, a senior partner in the firm intervened. "Hire him," he declared. "He's a Mormon stake president; he won't steal from us." Integrity is the jewel in the crown of character!

LOVE

Love has been mentioned often in this book. No wonder; the theme of love runs like a golden thread through the tapestry of the gospel. Jesus, the very embodiment of love, used it as the central principle of His teachings. To the lawyer who asked, "Master, which is the great commandment in the law?" Jesus replied, "Thou shalt love the Lord thy God with all thy heart, and with all thy soul, and with all thy mind. This is the first and great commandment. And the second is like unto it, Thou shalt love thy neighbour as thyself. On these two commandments hang all the law and the prophets." (Matthew 22:36–40.)

After the physiological needs for food, clothing, and shelter are met, humankind's greatest need is to be accepted, cared for, needed—to love and be loved in return. Those whose lives are deficient in this most important psychological need are unfulfilled and empty, sometimes becoming twisted and perverted.

Love is many things and, in the ultimate analysis, may be impossible to precisely define. In large measure the world has trivialized and degraded love as synonymous with lust or sex. It is, of course, much more. Christian love is characterized by unselfishness, by constancy, and by universality. Love, as Paul pointed out, "suffereth long, and is kind; . . . envieth not; . . . vaunteth not itself; . . . seeketh not her own, . . . rejoiceth not in iniquity, but rejoiceth in the truth." (1 Corinthians 13:4–6.)

Christians, if they are to follow Jesus' admonitions, must love everyone. "Ye have heard that it hath been said, Thou shalt love thy neighbour, and hate thine enemy. But I say unto you, Love your enemies, bless them that curse you, do good to them that hate you, and pray for them which despitefully use you, and persecute you; that ye may be the children of your Father which is in heaven." (Matthew 5:43–44.)

Of all the counsel given by Jesus, the admonition to love our enemies is, I think, the hardest to follow. The world over, blood feuds, many of them centuries old, attest to the proclivity of the natural man to strike out at real or imagined enemies. Such behavior is a horrifying affront to the God and Father of us all. It will be cured and prevented only by love. The covenant people of God must rid themselves of every vestige of hatred; they must love all men and women everywhere as their brothers and sisters. The truth is that we can run away from each other, we can even abuse and mistreat each other, but we cannot escape each other. Every soul on this planet is bound to us and we to them.

A 1983 made-for-television movie entitled *The Scarlet and the Black* portrayed vividly the conflict between good and evil in the world and the struggle of a good man to forgive and love his enemy.

In the movie, which is based on a true story, Gregory Peck played Monsignor Hugh O'Flaherty, an Irish Catholic priest assigned to the Vatican; Christopher Plummer portrayed his antagonist, Colonel Herbert Kappler, the head of the Gestapo in Rome during the German occupation of the city in World War II. From his base in the Vatican, which was declared neutral territory during the war, O'Flaherty ran an escape network throughout Rome for hundreds of Allied soldiers fleeing Nazi prison camps. For several months he and Colonel Kappler played a deadly cat-and-mouse game in which the Nazis attempted to lure O'Flaherty outside of the Vatican where he could be captured and have no recourse to diplomatic immunity. All attempts failed, to the intense frustration and murderous anger of Colonel Kappler and his superiors.

As the Allied armies advanced on Rome and the German soldiers began to withdraw, Kappler requested a private meeting with the priest:

O'Flaherty: "What is it you want from me, Kappler?"

Kappler: "They say that you can't pass a beggar or a lame dog, that you see yourself with some sort of obligation to look after anyone in trouble. You help British and American prisoners, Jews, Arabs, refugees, anybody. It's a part of your faith. Is that right?

O'Flaherty: "Well, I won't deny it. That is why I became a priest."

Kappler: "Brotherly love and forgiveness, that is the other half of what you believe, true?"

O'Flaherty: "True."

Kappler: "I am glad of it because I have three more for your mercy wagon—my wife and two children. If the partisans get them, they will be killed. I want them out of Rome and safe. That is what I want from you, Priest."

O'Flaherty: "You're asking me to save your family."

Kappler: "If you really believe what you preach you will do it."

O'Flaherty: "You expect me to help you after what you've done. You think you can demand forgiveness. You think it comes automatically because you want it."

Kappler: "I'm not talking about myself."

O'Flaherty: "You turned this city into a concentration camp. You've tortured and butchered my friends. You violated every principle of God and man. I can't believe after all you've done, you want mercy."

Kappler: "I told you, for my family."

O'Flaherty: "They're just part of you, part of what you stand for. They've taken whatever they could get without a thought for the suffering all around them, and now you demand that they be saved. I'll see you in hell first."

Kappler: "No, you are no different from anyone else. All your talk means nothing. Charity, forgiveness, mercy—it is all lies. You hear me, lies! Don't you talk to me about God and humanity. . . . There is no God, no humanity. You hear me, you hear me, Priest . . . Priest."

When Rome fell to the Allies, Kappler was captured. It was only during his interrogation that he learned his wife and children had indeed been aided and were safe in Switzerland. He was sentenced to life imprisonment for his war crimes. Kappler's only visitor in his Italian jail cell, once a month, year after year, was O'Flaherty. In 1959, the former Gestapo chief was baptized into the Catholic church at the hand of his former nemesis, the Irish priest.

One key aspect of Christian love is its unselfishness. The inspiring story of Donna Carson and of those who cared for her for over three decades illustrates both the unselfish nature of true love and the blessings that come to all, givers and receivers alike, who participate in it.

Shortly after being called to serve as a missionary in 1955, Donna was stricken with polio. Within days she was paralyzed from the neck down, with only limited use of three fingers on her left hand. For many years she was cared for by her loving parents and her brother and his wife. As her parents' health began to fail, hundreds of men and women, volunteers all, moved to provide Christ-like compassionate service. Because of her total helplessness, Donna required a great deal of assistance. At one time, more than forty people served regularly, six persons per day, seven days a week. Several priesthood leaders would take turns staying throughout the night, sleeping on a couch near Donna's bedroom so they could assist if she had difficulty breathing. On one occasion, she became comatose, and it was feared she would die. "We prayed her alive," one priesthood leader said. "We were afraid that if we didn't have her with us, selfishness would come back into our hearts." ("The Donna Carson Story: A Legacy of Love," *Ensign*, December 1992, p. 57.)

Why did so many help Donna? Their answers tell much about both the givers and the receiver:

"I came because I loved her."

"She was my friend."

"It was an honor. It was no imposition at all."

"I came away feeling as though I had served my Heavenly Father. And yet it was I who had been served. Donna gave and gave and gave until we were filled."

"We were blessed whenever we went. A special spirit abode there." (Ibid., pp. 56–57.) Sister Carson died in 1991, her earthly mission fulfilled—to help others grow closer to the Savior through service and to serve as an example of Christ-like love.

THE WEIGHTIER MATTERS OF THE LAW

Jesus pronounced woes on the scribes and Pharisees who had a "form of godliness but [denied] the power thereof." (See Joseph Smith–History 1:19.) "Woe unto you, scribes and Pharisees, hypocrites! for ye pay tithe of mint and anise and cummin, and have omitted the weightier matters of the law, judgment, mercy, and faith: these ought ye to have done, and not to leave the other undone." (Matthew 23:23.) Jesus, of course, was not protesting against men and women who paid their tithes and offerings. To do so is an essential part of obedience. The Savior, was, however, deeply concerned by those who carry out the rituals of religion while neglecting matters of greater importance.

Similar sentiments were expressed by the prophets of ancient Israel who saw in their societies tendencies to live by rote and ritual rather than by a deep and meaningful faith that leads to personal and societal righteousness. Speaking for God, Amos, the shepherd-prophet who lived eight centuries before Christ, proclaimed, "I hate, I despise your feast days, and I will not smell in your solemn assemblies. Though ye offer me burnt offerings and your meat offerings, I will not accept them: neither will I regard the peace offerings of your fat beasts. Take thou away from me the noise of thy songs; for I will not hear the melody of thy viols. But let judgment run down as waters, and righteousness as a mighty stream. . . . Seek ye me, and ye shall live." (Amos 5:21–24, 4.)

Micah, prophesying two generations after Amos, proclaimed the same theme: ritual is no substitute for personal goodness. "Will the Lord be pleased with thousands of rams, or with ten thousands of rivers of oil? Shall I give my firstborn for my transgression, the fruit of my body for the sin of my soul? He hath shewed thee, O man, what is good; and what doth the Lord require of thee, but to do justly, and to love mercy, and to walk humbly with thy God?" (Micah 6:7–8.)

Rote and ritual have their place, to be sure; but these great prophets counsel that we must also remember justice, mercy, humility, and obedience to the weightier matters of the law.

Latter-day prophets echo the same theme. "Please, priesthood brethren," said President Spencer W. Kimball, "do not get so busy trying to manage Church programs that you forget those basic duties . . . [which] the apostle James described as 'pure religion and undefiled' (James 1:27)." (*Ensign*, July 1979, p. 2.) Please understand. President Kimball, like the prophets before him, was not saying that programs are unnecessary or a waste of time. He was specifically reminding us that we can be very busy yet be neglectful of duties and responsibilities that lie at the very heart of Christian stewardship. Unless we are ever vigilant, our religious life can be reduced to a pattern of ritual and repetition, of unthinking habit that limits our vision and perspectives and will stunt our souls if unchecked. Such spiritual myopia is not pleasing to God or to his prophets.

A few years ago, a close associate shared with me a story that teaches much about the weightier matters of the law. My friend and his wife were required to visit his wife's parents, who were not in good health, in a faraway city. While they were gone from home, my friends left their family in the charge of their eighteen-year-old daughter, a capable and competent young woman. During the week they were gone, adversity struck. One of the boys in the family developed blood poisoning from an infected scratch on his leg and had to hobble around on crutches. A second son sliced his finger badly doing amateur woodworking; the youngest son broke a thumb playing softball. To top it off, the baby developed pneumonia.

The day before my friends were scheduled to return, the visiting teachers came around to the home. One stayed in the car, with the motor running, while the second sister rang the doorbell. "Is your mother home?" she inquired of the pitiful cast of walking wounded who opened the door. When told the mother was absent, the visiting teacher said, "Well, we just wanted to call, to make certain we got 100 percent visiting teaching this month. Have a good day!"

Significantly, the weightier matters of the law center on people and on their relationships with each other. What happens to people is what really counts in every situation and setting. Christ's atoning blood was shed to bless the lives of individual people and to enable them to return to their Father's home. The principles and ordinances of the gospel themselves—faith, repentance, baptism, and so on— derive their value and meaning because they build people into a Zion people. Even the Church itself exists to bless people. Man was not made for the Church; rather, the Church was made for man.

In His ministry, Jesus demonstrated repeatedly His great love for and total commitment to people—to the Exalted Man called Elohim whom we (and Jesus) refer to as Father—and to His brothers and sisters, including you and me. Jesus had a special love for the poor and the needy, the sick and the afflicted, those oppressed or in want. He comforted the poor, healed the leper, fed the hungry, and raised the dead. We who aspire to become the Zion people of God, a "peculiar treasure" unto Him, must seek always to emulate the Savior's example, and with love and integrity do all in our power to "bear one another's burdens, that they may be light; . . . mourn with those that mourn; yea, and comfort those that stand in need of comfort." (Mosiah 18:8–9.)

EPILOGUE

The vision of a Zion society, whose framer and finisher is God, is a powerful motivational force for humble disciples of Christ. It lifts and inspires them to do better; to strive, struggle, and endure; to move upward to new plateaus of righteousness. It draws them closer to Christ, the perfect, sinless Son of God; the Great Exemplar; the Way and the Truth. They wear out their lives in service to Him. They feel deeply the power of His atonement as it works a miracle of change in them. They become as little children and as Saints of God.

Their labors and efforts are full of gladness and rejoicing. Their hearts are "brim with joy" (Alma 26:11); putting aside the selfishness of the natural man, they seek the success and welfare of others above their own. They labor to bring other souls to taste of the "exceeding joy of which [they] did taste" that others, too, might also be "born of God and be filled with the Holy Ghost." (Alma 36:24.)

Although almost all attempts to establish Zion have failed, we must ever cling to the dream of the better world it promises. If Zion is to be redeemed, we must work harder than ever before, pray more diligently, hold ever sacred the covenants we have made with God, struggle each day that we live to cleanse our souls of selfishness, and labor always for Zion and her cause. Only as we become a people pure in heart and in deed will Zion "arise and shine in splendor amid the world's deep night." (*Hymns,* no. 40.)

Index